PRISON

ISBN 978-0-557-15507-1

PRISON

Twenty-Five Years as a New York State Correction Officer

Chris Leo

"Unless they wore the uniform, no matter who tries to explain the job of a Correction Officer, they will always fail and they will never do it justice."

Chris Leo –Correction Sergeant (Retired)

Table of Contents

Forward

What's a good day working in a New York State prison? When my fellow officers and I walk back out through those iron gates at the end of our shift without injury, and go home to our loved ones. Other than police, fire and the military can you imagine saying goodbye to your family each day and not knowing if you will be alive at dinner time?

Nowadays, almost everyone has a good idea of how prisons operate from watching the many television shows dedicated to this topic. Yes, we walk amongst, stand beside, and are surrounded by murderers, sex offenders, burglars and thieves, alcoholics and drug users, and any other violent crime you read about. We watch over them all.

Correction Officers have inmate's feces and urine thrown on us; we are spit on, assaulted, stabbed and even murdered. From my experiences, the average citizen is sincerely interested when they ask the question "What prison is like?" They want to know what its like behind those large concrete walls and razor ribbon fences.

As one imagines, prison is years of routines, which almost everyone is familiar with from popular television shows and specials; such as "Lockup."

I looked back over my twenty-five year career and have compiled stories that stood out as not being within the confines of the "routine." These stories are in no way the norm, but as you can imagine, strange things do happen in prison.

This is not a book from the abstract world of academia where those that have never worked in a prison tell those of us that do how it "should" work.

This is a book of what actually happens.

New York State prisons are operated far differently than many of the prison television shows would indicate from other states. New York's inmates are rarely in their cells. The prisons in New York operate under an "open" or "program oriented" system. Other than to sleep and to be counted, the inmates are freely walking about in the 16 maximum security prisons all day, every day. In the medium security prisons, of which there are approximately 30,000 inmates currently, the inmates are never locked in at all. They can't be. Why? In New York's 37 medium security prisons and 13 minimum security prisons there are no cells, no doors and no bars. What does this mean? It means that if and when there is a problem, of which we have many, there is no place to lock the inmates in. I guess you can always tell them to go back to their cubes. The inmates live and sleep in dormitory style settings. Why is this important?

The administration remains focused on programs and rehabilitation and unfortunately, pay's more attention to the calculator than security.

The New York State department of corrections likes to speak in simplistic terms when they casually discuss the security staffing ratio of New York prisons. Keep in mind they do this while sitting in the comfort and safety of their offices far away from the inmates. With all the very well compensated people in their Albany administration building the best they have come up with is taking the total number of inmates and dividing that by the total number of Correction Officers. Sixty-thousand inmates divided by nineteen-thousand officers. This archaic abacus minded scheme would lead the public and press to believe that there is a 3:1 ratio. Since most of the administrators we deal with have never worked in a security capacity they fail to realize that although the inmates are there every day and all day for their entire sentences. Correction Officers work eight hour shifts and then go home. We take vacations from time to time, we have days off, we do occasionally get sick etc… All nineteen-thousand of us are not there all day and every day as their ratio equation would imply. The average Correction Officer in New York State watches approximately sixty (60) inmates or more by him or herself. Regrettably, we have not had a commissioner in quite some time that ever wore the uniform or has performed any security functions.

A Correction Officer

No one grows up thinking they want to be a correction officer and work in a prison. None of us naturally gravitates towards working within the confines of concrete walls, steel bars and razor sharp fences. No one wants to go to work every day for the next 25 years only to be surrounded by hundreds of convicted violent felons.

We correction officers don't begin our careers as unsociable, but we do finish that way. We enter that cold world trusting most and then learn that to trust no one is to trust everyone equally. We step into a world like none other and never even realize that our career has just shortened our life expectancy by about 20 years. We look into the eyes of thousands of evil people and not only learn to deal with them, but also how to sense evil in others. We learn to control and deny emotions. We are warriors who can never let down our guard or we lose the edge. Losing that edge can create a situation where we lose our lives.

Our world teaches us to look at everyone suspiciously, that most are trying to con us in some way or another, and that everyone has forgotten what we do to keep them safe 24 hours a day, 365 days a year. We are the most essential element of the any criminal justice system, yet the most misunderstood.

The Training Academy

This is what the department of corrections officially states:

Correction Officer Trainees with the New York State Department of Correctional Services are required to participate in, and satisfactorily complete, all requirements of a 12-month training program before they can advance to the position of Correction Officer. As part of this program, Correction Officer Trainees are required to attend the Correctional Services Training Academy for a minimum of eight weeks of formal training. Training at the academy includes academic courses in such areas as emergency response procedures, interpersonal communications, legal rights and responsibilities, security procedures, and concepts and issues in corrections. While at the academy, Correction Officer Trainees will be trained in defensive tactics, use of handcuffs and other physical restraints, use of a baton, use of chemical agents, use of firearms, and use of physical and deadly physical force. Correction Officer Trainees will also receive rigorous physical training to develop fitness, strength and stamina while attending the academy. Upon graduating from the academy, Correction Officer Trainees are sworn in as New York State Peace Officers and are issued their shield and identification card. After graduating from the academy, Correction Officer

Trainees will receive three weeks of field training at a maximum-security correctional facility. Blah , Blah , Blah.

The New York State Correction Academy is located just outside the city of Albany in Colonie, New York. There are some people who work at the Academy whose intentions are good, but most of the positions are filled with those who are there only to prove their worth to someone higher than them. This way, they can be "taken care of" and not have to work in the prisons forever. It's kind of like kissing the ring in the mafia except here they have those that kiss lower on the anatomy. If they pay enough attention to the lower posterior, they may get their shot at becoming one of the very well compensated administrators who work in the department of corrections colossal command center a few miles away.

At the state office campus on Washington Avenue, there is a massive operations center filled with these types of self-important people—the bureaucrats who have never even seen an inmate in their careers or those who were never involved with quelling a violent situation in a prison. But you can be damn sure they will be the first to tell you how you should have handled the situation-after the fact.

The department of corrections imposes many rules and harsh penalties on security staff for the silliest of reasons. Sometimes, if you turn around quickly, you

12

can see them chuckle as they suspend an officer for some trivial violation of their infinite rules. There are 379 directives in the New York State Department of Corrections alone and that doesn't even include the Employee's Manual that they will enforce when it fits their needs. Only 36 of the 379 directives deal with security services.

You might ask yourself, why so many rules in the department of corrections? Here is the simple answer: As each of the egotists move up the chain of command and gets a higher rank, they have more of a need to validate how they got the promotion. Deep down even they know they did not earn these positions by working in the areas with inmates. However, with their ability to not get involved with incidents, they have impressed the administration enough that they become the safe choice. Fighting both the demons within and their ego, they start to believe in themselves. Typically, these individuals are the types that used to get beat up in the schoolyards and now they have the capacity to do something about it. They have crossed over to the dark side. This is a side where you no longer discipline inmates. Now you discipline staff as they devise new ways to go "easier" on the inmates.

The only way to announce their newly found authority and false sense of self-worth is to write memos. Just like a male dog marking new territory with urine, the administrators in DOCS write memo after memo for the smallest of matters. They lift their leg and mark anything they can think of, masking any unfamiliar odors with their own scent. And because all the real issues have already been taken care of, they have to become creative. We had this one idiot write a memo to alert us to the fact that he was going on vacation and that he would let us know when he returned to duty. You guessed it—via a memo! All, I say all; topics are covered by mounds and mounds of directives. So the only way for these newly appointed suits to validate their promotions and salaries is to write, revise and sign memos. We have been lucky so far though; to date we are currently allowed to wipe ourselves in any manner we want after using the bathroom. If you ever want to know who has depleted the rain forest, check the amount of paper used by the New York State Department of Corrections.

My favorite is Directive 9999, which is titled, the Alphabetic Index of Directives by Subject. Keep in mind there is already Directive 0000, which is the Table of Contents, recently "marked" by the newly hired Osborne McKay for the newly created position of Deputy-Commissioner. He "marked his new territory" on July 1, 2009 by updating the table of contents. I told you they are very creative.

Six weeks in the academy is nothing more than the department of corrections telling you what they have to, in order to avoid lawsuits, and what you can't do as a Correction Officer. You learn how to fill out forms and how you should avoid using any physical force on the inmates. Then you learn how to do more paperwork. It's only when you get to your training facility that the real learning begins. That's when you realize that watching and observing inmate behavior is more important than if your nametag is properly affixed to both shirt and jacket. That's when you realize that many of the things you were exposed to at the academy were strictly for record keeping and will never be used. And that's when you realize that many of the "tough guys" who taught you at the academy were the punks at their assigned facilities.

I was eighteen and newly out of high school and into the New York State Correctional training academy in Albany, in January 1982. This was back in a time when the law allowed an 18-year-old kid to become a correction officer. The age limit was lowered to meet the rapidly increasing inmate population as well as the lack of people taking the exam to become correction officers. A few years later the age requirement was raised to the age of 21, where it had been.

Obviously, I had no idea what I was getting myself into when I signed up. After six weeks in the academy, I was assigned to Green Haven Prison located in Dutchess County, New York. It's a maximum security prison made famous by the murder of Correction Officer Donna Payant, which took place only a matter of months before I began my career. She was killed by inmate Lemuel Smith, who I later came in contact with when I transferred to both Downstate and Elmira correctional facilities.

On my first day some 25 years ago, the Captain that gave us our orientation began with, "Anyone here under 21 years of age, raise your hand." We had gone through the same crap at the Training Academy in Albany and we already knew what he was going to say. The "old-timers" were not very excited with all us "young kids" working alongside of them, as they so gently put it. "You should all rethink your career choice right now. I don't know who in Albany thought this was a good idea, but they fucked up and they're feeding you youngins to the wolves."

I will never forget that speech. Here was a guy on our side and he was basically saying he didn't want us there. By the way, who uses the word "youngins"? Some old geezer he was.

What the Hell Is That?

We went on our tour of the prison and when we got to A-block, it was explained to us that part of this block housed inmates in protective custody. The tour guide, saying he would return for us later, had some of us remain on A-block for a while. It was there that, suddenly, this "female" inmate appeared. She had her hand on her hip and a bandana tightly wrapped around her head. Her shirt was tied around her waist to show off her fake cleavage. She was the porter, which is an inmate chosen by the block officer, whose primary duties are general cleaning of the block and passing out of supplies. This porter sashayed around the tier as if "she" were the housemother of a college dorm. The overemphasized hand movements and the swishing of her hips showed everyone, more than just us, that "he" wanted to be acknowledged and treated as a female.

He walked toward our group, looked us over and said, "What are you all looking at?"

His higher pitched voice forced one of our group members to ask, "What the hell is that?"

Remember, many of us were fresh out of high school and this was long before cable TV or the Internet. None of us had previously been exposed to this rare social phenomenon. Seeing our first transvestite or "he/she" was not as common as it is today. We had been told about these things in the Academy, but it's still a very strange sight for an upstate 18- year-old boy, but this was only the beginning of things to come over the next 25 years. We all laughed as the senior officer said loudly, "That, my young lads, is Madeline and 'he' is the block porter."

Our tour continued and we were later escorted up the stairs to a reception unit on the next tier. There were over 100 inmates up there who had been transferred from Clinton prison located in Danemora, New York, because of a hunger strike. They were complaining about their arrival phone calls. According to the directive, they were supposed to get an arrival phone call within 24 hours of being transferred to a new facility. This way, they can let their family and friends know where they are. On the surface it makes sense, but making it happen isn't always that easy. Especially when arranging phone calls for 100 of them. Limited time, limited phones and one officer are not a good mix to accomplish such a large task.

But here we were and we had no idea what was going on. In the training academy they told us we would never see a sergeant unless it was a true emergency and all of a sudden, there was the first sergeant and then the second sergeant appeared. We were whispering among ourselves, "Wow two sergeants? This must be big."

The inmates were screaming and banging on their bars for their phone call. Their arms were reaching and swinging out of the bars, trying to get someone's attention. They were even yelling at us.

"Hey, you new jacks. Don't just stand there, you dumb honkies—get us our mother-fuckin' phone calls now!"

We all just stood there and looked at each other. We actually thought we were going to have to fight on our first day. But then, suddenly, the screaming and banging subsided. The inmates were quietly passing a message among themselves to quiet down and knock it off. Thinking back on it now, it was similar to when one animal in the herd can sense there is something dangerous approaching.

We didn't know what they were saying until we saw a third sergeant appear from around the corner. He had on this crisp white shirt with hair that hung down past his shoulders. He also had the cockiest way about him. And as he approached, we could make out what the inmates were saying to each other. They were saying things like, "Shhh, it's Farrell," and "Yo, knock it off, that's Farrell."

We looked at each other and watched as this cocky sergeant walked right by all of us, almost like a general on a horse preparing for battle. He then walked past each inmate and looked directly in each of their cells, staring at them as he passed, almost daring them to say something in his presence. As they became aware that he was there, they stopped their complaining altogether.

"Who is that guy?" one of us asked.

"That's Sergeant Farrell," answered one of the other sergeants. He said it in a tone that made us feel as if they were a little jealous of the respect he commanded.

Sergeant Farrell had walked about half way down the tier where one inmate continued to wave his arm outside the bars of his cell. Everyone else had stopped yelling so it was easy to hear what was going on.

"I don't give a fuck who you are, honky! I want my mother-fuckin' phone call," the inmate shouted.

Farrell stared the inmate in the eye and said, "You have one second to pull your arm inside your cell."

"Or else what?"

As quickly as that inmate uttered those words, questioning the consequences of what would happen, we heard a loud snapping noise echo down the stunned and quieted tier. Sergeant Farrell had effortlessly grabbed the inmate's wrist and, using the bars as a vice, pushed the locked elbow against the steel bars until it broke.

The inmate was now screaming, but this time in pain. "He broke my fuckin' arm! He broke it! He fuckin' broke it!"

A bunch of us looked at each other in shock and awe. I whispered to a guy I was friends with from the academy, "I thought they told us we couldn't touch the inmates? That guy just broke his arm."

We could overhear the other inmates telling the inmate with a now broken arm, "We told you that was Farrell. That guy is no joke."

We all wanted to know who this guy was. At the academy, we were taught about the new "hands off" policy. We were taught not to get physical or confrontational with the inmates. According to our instructors we had entered the department of corrections at a time referred to as the "New Corrections." In the event we did have to use physical force to protect ourselves, we had been taught that there would be piles of paperwork awaiting us and yet Farrell just walked away and didn't do anything. This was a sergeant everyone now wanted to work with.

Over the years, Sergeant Bruce Farrell and I became close friends. Through our many conversations I learned that the guys he started with from the 1960s and '70s had been around during the hostile takeover at Attica, and they were not going to let that happen again. They were used to doing whatever it took to get the job done. Consequently, they were in a strange place. There was a changeover going on from the old prison ways to the "new correction" ways. This was a tough and awkward transition period for the guys who, just like him, had experienced the worst that prison offered. Now Albany and the kindler, gentler corrections department wanted them to change how they handled things. These were the warriors of old and these new ways were foreign to them. There was no academy when they began their careers. They were given a set of keys and a baton and told, "Okay, go to work."

We had been trained that the new way was all about communication, not force. Now, on the job, we found that the six weeks at the academy did not prepare us properly at all. The academy concentrated so much on what they called interpersonal communication or IPC. They used this term so much that it became a joke. And as we put these IPC skills to the test, the inmates realized things were changing. But just like the old-timers, we were stuck between what we learned at the academy, what the senior officers were teaching us, and the way the inmates were responding to our "communication skills." We would watch the senior guys handle things and they would just laugh at the new and improved ways, as it was taught to us at the academy.

A few weeks later we were on our own and I was taking a count of the inmates. For fun, the inmates often attempt to distract you from the count by talking or creating a commotion in their cell. And when you are counting over 100 inmates to confirm they are all still there, the last thing you want to do is go back and start counting all over.

Well, on this particular time, I was on A3 tier and an inmate from A5 tier above yelled out, "Yo, C.O., you got the time?" So like a rookie I looked at my watch and using my new IPC skills said, "9:15."

He replied, "No, not that time, the time to suck my dick."

Everyone on the whole block, which had all been quiet during the count, laughed their asses off. It was somewhat funny and I laughed at it myself, too, but my learning experience of 25 years had officially begun.

Mess Hall in Prison

The first time I escorted inmates to the mess hall was on my second day. I was told by my A-Officer to take the inmates from tier 3 and 5 to chow. I walked up the stairs and began unlocking the cells of all the inmates who were eligible to attend the meal. I gave the order by yelling out, "On the chow."

The inmates already knew it was time to eat, without needing me to call out and thus, they began filing down the stairs and lining up. Once everyone was out, I had to run up and down each tier, making sure there were no lurking inmates in their cells who could rummage through other inmates cells. There were 50 cells on each side and my goal was to make sure that they were all secured before we left. An inmate is not obligated to go to the mess hall if they do not want to, and the last thing I needed was to have some inmate out of his cell and running around while I was in the mess hall.

After what felt like I was taking too long and hearing inmates in line making comments like, "Come on C.O. You're holding up my meal," I slammed the final cell shut. Knowing the two tiers I was responsible for were secured, I gave the order for them to proceed towards the mess hall. Luckily they knew where the mess hall was because I had no idea. There was a yellow line that the inmates

24

knew not to cross over as they walked, but it was more like a mob that I was just following.

Once in the mess hall I was told by the sergeant at the door what post I was to cover. "Have you ever been in the mess hall before?" he asked.

I told him no and said, "Second day." Thinking back, he must have seen an 18-year-old officer who was of no help to him entering one of the most dangerous areas of the prison. It was obvious by the way he rolled his eyes at me. I know this now because that's what I thought the many times I had a rookie assigned to me over the years.

There were quite a few of us new officers at that time and as we went to our posts, the sergeant pointed out that inmates were bringing glass bottles of spices, such as RedHot sauce, to the mess hall. This was not allowed, but it was a rule that had not been enforced over the years. The administration was beginning a crack down on this practice and the sergeant told us to begin collecting the bottles off the tables.

As I grabbed the small bottles from the tables I will never forget how quickly the realization of where I was set in. Approximately 500 inmates were collectively getting upset over the bottle collection, and they all began banging their silverware on the steel tables. They were not shouting anything, just banging in unison like something out of a James Cagney prison movie. I had no idea how serious it was until I looked around and saw that there were only six other officers and one sergeant in the area, and he was near the door.

The noise was so loud and we were so outnumbered that the sergeant walked up to each of us and said, "Give the bottles back."

I looked at him, confused, and said, "I don't remember who I took these from."

"Give them to whoever takes them," he said and then he yelled over the banging noise for everyone to settle down.

We quickly returned all the bottles and the noise stopped, but the inmates had won that round. Prison is dangerous enough and, my fellow officers and I were put in a dangerous situation by the incompetence of our superiors—incompetence of administrators making arbitrary decisions that could have resulted in a mess hall riot. This was my first experience of how quickly the department will give in to the inmates and how inadequate their plan of action is for things like this.

C.O., My Lights Don't Work

A few weeks later I had been assigned to the protective custody (PC) unit at Green Haven. The PC unit was separated and isolated from the general population by only a plexiglass shield in the middle of the tier. The general population inmates, whom we call GP, would constantly try to pass food or other items to the inmates in PC. The reason for this was that the PC inmates were limited in the amount of personal belongings they could keep in their cells and the GP inmates would charge them for any additional items they needed. I was given strict instructions by the senior officer that nothing , and I mean nothing, gets past that plexiglass gate into PC from GP or vice versa.

Of course, during my first time serving the meals to the PC inmates I was tested and it turned into a problem. One Italian inmate was now housed in PC because he had been "burned out" in his GP cell. An anonymous inmate had tossed a plastic bag of gasoline on his bed and blanket as he slept and with the flick of a match, this set him on fire. The visible damage to his face arms and hands was quite extensive. His hands had been burned so badly that they looked like two large hams attached to his forearms. I can't even imagine what the burning of skin must have smelled like.

The administration placed the badly burned inmate in "involuntary protective custody" for his own safety. So I was dealing with some inmates who wanted to be in PC and others who didn't want to be there at all. This inmate didn't want the stigma or negative reputation of being in PC. He didn't want to be there and made it clear every time I passed his cell.

There were no inmate porters allowed in PC for security reasons. Therefore, the officer assigned to PC had to dispense the meals from a cart. The meals were scooped from a heated cart in front of the inmate and the portions were all the same.

On this day the Italian inmate wanted to both test me and impress me. He was in the third cell on the PC tier, so he was very close to the gate leading to the GP cells. He had arranged, by yelling, for a GP inmate to pass him a loaf of bread when I opened the gate to push the feed-up cart into the PC side. I told the GP inmate, "No," as I locked the steel gate behind me.

Of course ham hands, being so close to the gate, overheard heard me and began pleading his case. "Hey C.O. Leo, it's okay, the other C.O.s do it all the time."

That is something I heard thousands of times in my career, but this was my first time. I repeated the rule, "Nothing passes through that gate."

He replied with, "You can check it. It's just bread."

As he was pleading, I was running through my head all the stuff we had learned in the academy about weapons being smuggled in food or that the bread could be poisoned, so I simply said, "No." Inmates, just like children, don't ever want to hear the word "no."

By then I was directly in front of his cell, preparing his portions while he observed my every movement. He caught my attention and said, "Leo, you gave the other guy more mash potatoes than you gave me."

I ignored him and continued preparing his meal.

Then he said, "You can give my pudding to ten cell because I don't want it."

I looked at him and said, "I will give you what you are supposed to get and you can pass your own pudding. I don't care how you get it to him, but I'm not passing it for you."

"You don't care, motherfucker," was all I heard when he threw the pudding bowl in my direction. It hit the bars and bounced back at him. His ham-hands

29

didn't help his accuracy at all. He had pudding all over him and I couldn't help but to break into laughter.

Well, this really made the little guy really angry and he reached for a jar of water with both of his stumpy hands. Back then the inmates would put just enough water in a glass jar so that when they threw it, the water would propel the broken shards of glass through the bars. This created a better chance of having the broken pieces of glass embed themselves into the victim's skin. And this time, I was the intended victim.

Instinctively, as he hurled the jar, I turned by back and immediately felt broken pieces of glass hitting me and saw them landing past me. Now my back was wet and I didn't know if it was from water or blood. I left the cart there and walked off the tier to check myself. It only takes one inmate or incident to rile the group and by this time, the rest of the 25 the PC inmates were throwing glass jars out of their cells. Some were just joining in for fun and some were angry that their food was now ruined on the cart with broken glass in it.

The senior officer must have heard the commotion and came down through the cat walk. The cat walk is a secured walkway behind the cells. He reached me as I was checking my back for blood and said, "What the hell happened?"

I began to explain the events that led to this mess. He stopped me and said, "Don't worry about this, rookie. Come with me."

He led me down the same cat walk he had just used to reach me and said, "Look," as he pointed. He showed me the panel behind the cells that had the access to each individual cell's plumbing and electricity. He walked down to ham-hands' cell and unscrewed the fuse for the electricity, and then did the same for every cell on the PC tier. Suddenly, the noise stopped.

"Yo, C.O., my lights don't work," the inmates called out.

"I know, I turned them off," he replied.

We now walked around to the front of the cells and he told them, "This officer now knows where the fuses are. It's up to him to turn them back on. I'm sure he will base his decision on your behavior. Now one of you assholes will volunteer to come out and clean all this up. And since you were all throwing glass, all of you can get written up or skip your meal. Skip your meal and we will call it even, because I'm not calling the mess hall and telling them I need a new meal for 25 assholes who wanted to ruin their own food. Does everyone agree?"

Not one inmate argued with him and that was that. One of the inmates volunteered to come out and sweep up all the glass and empty the food cart. Ham-hands actually called me over and apologized for acting the way he did and said, "I know you were only doing your job."

I later screwed the fuses back in and never had another problem while on that unit. Addressing the problem this way quickly solved it and with no paperwork. The academy way would have had me writing reports for the next two days. (A side note: Glass of any kind was eventually eliminated a few years later from the New York State correctional system, including the Red-Hot bottles.)

Water Torture?

As you can imagine, night time is the most peaceful part of each day in prison. Sure, we get the occasional inmate hanging himself in his cell or a heart attack here and there, but for the most part, the inmates are in their cells and depending on what prison you work at, there is a set time when all noise stops. This is called quiet time. Since Downstate is a reception prison, the quiet time starts a little earlier than other prisons.

At Downstate the noise stopped at 9:00pm each evening. There were always some inmates that would play cards or chess with the inmate in the next cell, and I normally let that continue if they were quiet and not bothering anyone. But there were always those inmates who wanted to test how far they could push the rules. They would also test how quickly we would confront them as they showed other inmates that they were willing to push back against the system.

On one particular night, I made my first announcement that it was quiet time at 9:00. Then I gave the inmates on the block a few minutes to say their good nights to one another. You would swear you were listening to an episode of *The Walton's*. The only difference is instead of, "Good night, John Boy," it's more like, "Good night, Son," "See ya in the morning, Slim," or "May Allah be with you, Yusef." You get the idea.

Once all the false niceties were finished there were maybe one or two inmates who tried to continue their conversations. Some of them were in cells right next to one another and some were from different ends of the block. As you can imagine, the acoustics on a prison cellblock are terrible. The noise bounces off the concrete floors and steel doors like hollow caverns. I can't tell you how many headaches I've left work with over the years because of the acoustics. Between the yelling of inmates, the banging of bars and the blaring of the television, it's almost like being at an Italian dinner where each person talks louder than the next in order for the others to hear you.

For those inmates in cells right next to each other, I tried to be fair and reminded them to keep it to a whisper and wrap it up quickly. But for the ones yelling and disturbing everyone else, I had to put a stop to it immediately. I almost always gave a warning first, but sometimes this kindness was taken as a weakness. Like lions sensing the weak or wounded in a herd, inmates will eat you up before you know what happened.

When the warning did not work or I got the occasional, "Fuck you," response, I simply opened the utility room that was located on the same tier as the talker or talkers. The tier was shaped in semi-circle shape and the inmates could watch your every movement. Once in the utility room, which was referred to as a "slop sink'" in prison, I took one of the metal mop buckets and strategically placed it upside down underneath the water faucet. After some experimentation I found that perfect angle where the water would make the loudest noise as it splashed against the galvanized steel of the bucket. I used enough water so that you heard each drop hit the bucket over the sound of the dripping. This got their attention quickly. It only took a few seconds for the talking inmate to ask, "Hey C.O., what is that for?"

"I told you and warned you to knock off the talking after I announced quiet time and you didn't understand that, so maybe you will understand this." Drip. Splash. Drip. Splash. Drip.

This technique always worked and the water only had to hit the bucket for a few minutes before the inmate would call me back to his cell and agree to stop talking. He either didn't want to hear the noise of the water or deal with the much larger inmate, who was trying to sleep, the next morning when the cell doors would open for chow.

I only did that a few times and only as a last resort, but it was quite effective.

The Captain Wants to See You   (Evaluation and Sick Time)

Every new officer has to complete a probationary period of one year. On many occasions, supervisors who never even work with officers review their performance. Typically, the administration will disregard anything positive on performance evaluations and only concern themselves with the negatives when it suits them. I have seen officers with 20 years of outstanding evaluations make one mistake and be severely penalized or even terminated without regard for the previous 19 evaluations.

At the age of 19, my first year as a correction officer was now completed. A sergeant that I had barley worked with called me to his office, handed me my final evaluation, and congratulated me on becoming a permanent officer. This was the first time I had ever seen this official document in person, so I looked over the many categories that my first year of work was being evaluated on. My attention was drawn to the only box that had been checked, "needs improvement." I was puzzled and a bit taken back. The title for that section read: Time and Attendance.

I inquisitively asked the sergeant what this meant and thought that maybe someone had made a mistake. He took the form back from my hands and looked it over again. He said that he had not actually prepared the evaluation himself and was not sure why the box was checked with such a negative rating. I later found out that there was actually a lieutenant whose only function at each prison in the state was to monitor all security staff time and attendance. The lieutenant had filled out the attendance section prior to giving it to the sergeant to then give to me.

Looking it over again, I noticed that the comment section recommended that I be placed on "time monitoring." This would mean that each time I was absent because of a sick day, I would have to go to a doctor and get a note to prove I was ill. In my first full year I had only used two days of sick time. If anything I should have at least received a "good."

I remember it well when the sergeant looked back at me and said, "Just sign the evaluation, it doesn't mean anything."

I replied that I was concerned with this being in my personal history folder on a permanent basis. I also told him I did not feel this was an accurate depiction of my first full year.

Rolling his eyes he handed me a pen and motioned again for me to just sign it. Knowing I was now permanent no matter what happens at this point, since the full year had passed, I told him that I didn't feel comfortable signing it until that time and attendance negative rating was at least re-evaluated. I was very confused because when the New York State Department of Corrections advertised the job of correction officer in the newspaper to get people to take the civil service exam, they touted the benefits of "twelve (12) paid sick days per year." Earning your sick time is part of the compensation package, similar to vacation time. You earn four hours of sick time per two-week pay period or eight hours (one day) per month.

What they don't tell any of the perspective applicants is that even though each officer earns those four hours per two-week pay period, DOCS does not want correction officers to use their earned sick time—ever. The department refuses to hire adequate security staffing, so they will harass and question every occasion of sickness to make up for their lack of proper staffing.

The sergeant called me back to his office later that afternoon and informed me that the day shift Captain wanted to see me. "He wants to discuss your refusal to sign the evaluation."

Going to see a captain is tantamount to being ordered to see the principle in high school. For having been out of high school for only one year now, I was beginning to wonder if this was how all adults behaved at work, or was it only in civil service?

"The Captain will see you now," his secretary said as she escorted me into a well-furnished office. I walked in with a smile on my face because this was the first time I was meeting a captain and because I saw the bottle of Vodka he was trying to place behind some books as I entered. He remained seated when I walked in he didn't say anything, so I walked toward the empty chair in front of his desk and started to sit down.

"Did I tell you that you could sit down, son?" he said, making me snap back up on my feet. I thought to myself, Uh oh, he's and asshole like they said he was. The older officers had advised me he was just an old drunk that loved power so much that he refused to retire even though he was eligible years ago.

"Son, do you have a problem with authority?" he asked in a gruff voice.

I wanted to badly say, Hey asshole, I'm not your son and this has nothing to do with authority, but I respected the rank and I was new, so I just said, "No."

He stood up and came slowly from behind his desk to stare me down. "Then why is it when a sergeant tells you to sign a form, you refuse to do so?" The smell of alcohol was so strong on his breath that I had to turn my head. .

"Sir, I didn't refuse. I asked about the time monitoring section and the remarks. I thought there was a mistake and wanted it checked out. I only used two days of sick time in the whole year."

He was one of those captains that looked right through officers as if he was more concerned with the wall behind them than talking to them. Raising his voice he said, "Only two days? Son, is that how you look at it? We look at as two days where someone else had to work in your place. We have to hire overtime because you are not here. That sick time is only for emergencies."

Again, only being 19 years old, my responses were not as well thought out as they are today, but that was back then and I had less experience. I muttered, "Sir, I only called in sick on those two days." I was really thinking that only a year ago I was working at Burger King and would call in sick every Friday and Saturday night just to go hang out with my friends. Now I only used two days in a whole year and I have some asshole fire breather angry that I used two of the twelve sick days I legally earned.

"Son, I'll tell you what I'm gonna do. Since you are so inquisitive I'm going to have you talk to the supervisor that prepared your evaluation. This way you can discuss your hesitation to sign with him directly."

I then said to myself, Wow this captain is not that bad, but as I approached the door to leave, the captain said, "Officer Leo—by the way, the sergeant that did your evaluation works on the midnight shift. So we will be changing your shift and you will be on midnights the next few weeks. This way you can get your questions thoroughly answered. Have a nice day and close my door when you leave."

I closed his door and whispered, "What an asshole."

"I didn't hear that," his secretary said.

Slowly, I walked back to the real job of watching inmates. I had finally just gotten settled into the day shift from the afternoon shift and now Captain Kangaroo puts me on midnight the shift. The worst shift of all to me. Some officers do their whole careers on midnights, but that is not a shift for me.

After a few nights on the midnight shift, the sergeant came to my workstation and asked, "You the one that has problem with the evaluation I did?"

Frustrated at his question, I said, "It's not a problem, it's just a question."

"Okay. What's your question?"

"I just wanted to know why, with only two sick days, I received a "needs improvement" and also why, in the remarks, it recommends time monitoring."

"We're being told to come down hard on anyone using their sick time," the supervisor admitted. "I don't have your evaluation with me, but I'll look at it tomorrow and we can discuss it then."

Unfortunately, this overbearing and archaic management style HAS ONLY GROWN over my career and is still rampant in the department of corrections today. As a union representative I can confirm that this domineering and pompous style has CAUSED MORE PROBLEMS, builds resentment and always backfires.

I eventually signed the pointless document and a few months later was reassigned to the day shift. From this experience, I made it my mission to use as much sick time as possible throughout my career. The only good that came from of all of this was that I realized my fellow CO's were the only ones I could count on. My future was in hands of people who could care less about me.

So my second mission was to get a college degree as a way to mitigate against the tyrants who I now worked for. That supervisor didn't motivate me to save my sick time, but the situation did motivate me to go on and attain two college degrees in both criminal justice and political science. You see, DOCS intimidates the officers for one simple reason, to save on overtime. The prisons are so understaffed by security that they require large amounts of overtime to run safely. So as they attempt to cut the overtime by bullying correction officers into not using their sick time, they create a vicious cycle of exhausting the security staff to the point of using more sick time, hence more overtime.

If they ever hire the appropriate number of correction officers, they will accomplish proper security staffing levels and allow the officers to use their earned sick time. Ironically, the division of budget has already approved and appropriated the proper number of correction officers in New York. It's the administration that refuses to maintain that legal staffing level. Their official statement is that they seek safety and yet they themselves stand in the way of safe staffing.

So my advice to every officer I encounter is to use ALL your sick time before you retire. The life expectancy of a Correction Officer is 57 years of age.

Look at it like this—the more days you are away from the stress of the prison, the more you extend your life. On the day I retired in April 2007, I proudly had only 80 hours of accumulated sick time. That's in deep contrast to officers who have retired with 1600 hours of accumulated sick time. And here is the irony of all ironies: you read about complaints that are made daily about the overuse and the high cost of health insurance. So you would think that New York State would be aware that one of their own departments creates a vicious circle of forcing thousands of state employees to go the doctor simply to get a doctor's note in order to use their own earned sick time.

Lowest Rung

In the eyes of the New York State Department of Corrections, the correction officer is the lowest rung of the ladder. Of course, they will deny this, but if you want a real view of the organizational chart, ask a correction officer. The pecking order is as follows: administration, civilian staff, inmates and then correction officers.

The lack of respect for a correction officer is demonstrated daily when DOCS, from the comfort of a desk, will so casually assign one officer to watch 60 inmates by himself or herself. They close yard towers and put two or three officers in the yard with 300 inmates. On just one occasion we would love to see one of the suits come from behind his desk, walk out to the yard, and stand there with us. Once he is finished wetting his pants, maybe he would say, "Wow you guys need some help out here."

DOCS will always back their administrators even when they are wrong, because if they didn't, they would have to admit fault. Fault is a prohibited word for them. And under the current guidelines, DOCS does not have to provide any supporting documentation as to why they made a negative evaluation. Nor will they reverse a decision made by an administrative colleague.

In my long career of receiving performance evaluations and representing officers in disputing their performance evaluations, I can say that most negative evaluations usually stem from personality conflicts. Countless outstanding officers who I trusted with my life have experienced the same thing as well. We have many instances where an officer is an excellent officer, but the person doing the evaluation may not like him or her. The evaluations don't really do or mean anything, but they can be a source of pride. Prison is negative enough without someone reviewing your performance for the past year based on one incident or a personality conflict.

An officer can appeal an evaluation to his local administration, but that is like a child asking his father to side with him against his mother over a punishment. DOCS lives by an administrative slogan of "we administrator's must stand together." I have attended and represented many officers at the evaluation appeal "hearing." and I hear the same thing over and over. When I or the appealing officer asks for any documentation supporting a negative comment on the evaluation, the DOCS response is, "We are not required to provide that." If I or the appealing officer asks if the administration has anything that supports the "needs improvement" mark, whereas a year ago it was good or excellent, the response is, "We are not required to provide that." Then, if I or the appealing officer provides written statements from fellow officers that work in his immediate area on a daily basis directly negating a negative statement, the officer's statements are summarily dismissed as biased and not relevant or both.

As a union official I had to deal frequently with one cranky old woman civilian employee who used to serve on the agency evaluation appeal board. In one case, the officer I represented was appealing a poor rating in the "relationship with fellow employees" section. The officer had already appealed the annual grading at his local facility, and it was denied under the guise that there was no evidence to support his claim.

Once the appeal moved up to the next step, the "agency level," I asked the officer to have all the officers who work in his immediate area write and sign statements saying he gets along just fine with his fellow employees. He supplied me with ten written statements supporting his original appeal, which I then submitted at the agency level appeal. This civilian employee, who was a bean counter from the budget department, had the audacity to ask me, "How do we (the board) know you didn't write and sign these letters yourself?"

I shook my head and replied, "Are you that foolish to think I would sign letters and put myself in a in a forgery situation?"

These are the extents to which DOCS will go to protect their administration.

I only get to handle the evaluation appeals that continue to be pursued past the facility level hearings. These are the evaluation appeals that are appealed even further after the local administration go through the farce of conducting an appeal process and denies them. Most officers don't even bother with these appeals because they know their concerns will always be met with that big rubber stamp dripping wet with red ink that says, "DENIED." They use that stamp so much it doesn't get a chance to dry. Consequently, most officers don't want give the administration the satisfaction of using it.

I will admit that for a short time, there was extreme fairness when it came to an officer appealing an evaluation at the agency level. The reason the evaluation appeals became fair at the agency level was not because of the system, but because of one man—John Malloy, the Superintendent at the Academy prior to his retirement. Malloy was the only one who would actually be honest and fair when it came to these appeals. He even ignored that bitchy woman from the budget department when she piped in with her cranky remarks.

Based on his decisions, Malloy understood the fact that if an officer was taking the time to appeal the evaluation, there was probably something else going on. Historically, the evaluation appeal committee Mr. Malloy chaired would usually recommend upholding the facility recommendation. This meant denying the officers claim. Superintendent Malloy would take the time to investigate and even use his power as chairman of the committee to overrule their recommendations. He was the only person in that position who understood the morale value of employee evaluations. Unfortunately, Mr. Malloy retired a few years ago and his replacement was worse than could have been imagined. The new chairman of the evaluation appeal committee, as well as the committee members, might as well attach a rubber stamp to their hands that reads, "APPEAL DENIED." I wonder if they own stock at the red ink store?

Are You Guys Frigging Crazy?

A couple of years later I was working at Downstate Correctional facility in Fishkill, New York. It is a maximum security reception facility that most of New York's inmates pass through upon leaving their respective county jails. If a person is sentenced to one year or less, they complete their sentence at the county jail. One year or more they go to state prison.

Upon arrival, all inmates are stripped, frisked, searched and scanned with a metal detector. They are then assigned a department identification number (DIN #). They are showered and deloused. Each inmate receives a basic short haircut in accordance with department standards. All inmates are issued two sets of standard state inmate clothing, including two pair of green pants, two green shirts, set of white underwear, one pair of black work boot/sneakers and one pair of white socks.

Standard department identification photographs are then taken for the department ID card, and each inmate is fingerprinted. Each is seen by medical personnel and blood work is performed, along with more extensive medical tests, if warranted, to see if the inmate is bringing a disease or virus into the prison. A DNA sample is taken if the conviction is for a violent crime. If deemed necessary, some are interviewed by a department psychologist.

Following the initial reception process and security orientation, inmates are advised of the rules and regulations for New York State prisons.

Downstate used to be operated very strictly because of the quick processing nature. We would receive 100 or so inmates a day from New York County jail, Rikers Island , and then more would arrive from all the other county jails around the state. So when you are dealing with hundreds of inmates daily where you don't

know their backgrounds, personalities or tendencies, you have to treat them all the

same. In this case it was strict, like boot camp.

These inmates typically stay at Downstate Correctional facility for 30 days.

During this period they are cleaned up, given a uniform, a haircut and locked in for

most evenings until they are classified by a counselor. We had maximum, medium

and minimum security all mixed in together until they finished their testing. Also

like the military, each inmate is tested medically, psychologically and

educationally. This helps counselors decide where the inmate will be sent based

on the crime, sentence, medical or psychological condition, and what trade or

schooling he or she should or will pursue. Academic and IQ testing is also

performed on each inmate.

Keeping the maximum security inmates from harming the medium and

minimum security inmates during this intake period was difficult enough, but I'll

never forget this one captain who was new to Downstate and made our job much

more difficult. He was a Hispanic man who reminded me of Poncho Villa from the

movies I watched as a kid. He was new as a captain and had just transferred in

from a medium security prison. He made rank very quickly, which is always

suspicious. These guys are usually the ones who sell their soul to be where they are and sure enough he made his rank by helping create the DOCS Olympics. He was the king of those administrators I spoke about who use memos as way to reinforce their rank.

This genius had been there less than a month when he wrote a memo that said, "All inmates will be allowed out on Super bowl Sunday to watch the big football game." This, despite the fact that we had a 30-day rule, which said, "Inmates are required to wait 30 days for night recreation."

When we saw this, we officers were scratching our heads and quite angry, but we figured that maybe he wrote the memo without having someone with knowledge of reception procedures look it over first. Then our area supervisor told us that the clueless captain had indeed known about the 30-day rule for reception inmates, but wanted to give them a treat. So he wrote his memo that would allow the all reception inmates out to watch the game anyway.

The reason the inmates were required to wait 30 days for night recreation was twofold. First, we don't know what the inmates' security classification is until they have been assessed by the counselors. This 30-day period also gives the officers a chance to observe and learn the personalities of the new inmates before they are out at night when fewer staff members around. This brings me to my second point: The security staffing on the afternoon shift, which would be on duty during the game, is about one-third of the day shift, because the inmates are usually locked in. All administrative and civilian staff are finished and out of the prison at 4:00pm each day. In New York State prison, the prisons are run on skeleton crews even while the inmates are out going to the gyms, taking showers, watching movies, going to the barber shop etc.

As a result, the superintendent said they could hire an extra rounds man on Super Bowl Sunday to walk around and make sure everything was okay. I happened to be on the afternoon shift (3-11pm) during that time so I got a few of the other 3-11 officers together. Collectively and naively we thought that maybe if we write letters to the captain and explain why this is should not take place in a maximum security reception prison, maybe he would reverse his decision. I don't know if it was the anger that took the better of us, but the letters became something more and started to look like ransom notes you see on TV. The letters digressed from well-thought out ideas to very threatening letters that basically said he should leave and go back to a medium prison. That was a big mistake.

It was a Saturday night when we placed the "notes" in his mailbox, which was a wooden hinged contraption bolted to the wall and complete with a padlocked hasp. It looked more like a wooden safe fitted with a slot on the top that allowed mailed to be put inside.

The following day was Sunday and one week before the Super bowl. My buddy and I proudly told Sergeant Farrell, who was now at Downstate, what we had done. We were beaming with excitement in front of the legend himself, until he looked at us and smirked.

"Are you guys fringing crazy?" he said with his heavy Brooklyn accent. He then went on to scold us, "They will investigate those notes and you two will be fired. They have IG officers just sitting around on their asses waiting for things like this to look into. You threatened a captain?"

He continued to give it to us, shaking his head as he spoke. "Look, I don't like that ass kisser either, but you can't threaten him in writing. Go kick his ass in a bar or slash his tires, but do it in writing and they will come after you."

My buddy Paul and I looked at each other and our pride quickly became fear. The reality settled in quickly. We had both started this job at the age of eighteen, both had about two year's seniority by then, and now we realized we were in serious trouble.

Our scolding from Sgt. Farrell took place about ten feet from the secured lock box that now held our future. Sergeant Farrell thought about the situation and offered a way out. "Look, it's a weekend and you put those letters in the box last night, right?"

We nodded in the affirmative.

"The captain is off on weekends and won't open that box until tomorrow. That means you two idiots need to get all those letters out of that box today."

The line up and roll call was about to begin any minute but Farrell had our backs. "You two stay in this area during roll call. I will check you both in on the charts. I don't care how you do it, but get those letters out of that box," he said, still shaking his head in disbelief at what we had done.

The line up room was far enough away that no one would hear us breaking into the captain's mail box. We were lucky that not only had we told the only supervisor who could help us, but on a weekend, there is no other staff working to hear us clink and clank. If this was any other day we would have been fired for sure and my career would have been over after two short years.

We only had about fifteen minutes until the Watch Commander returned from roll call and his office was located directly in front of the mailbox we were about to break open. Paul and I quickly looked around for something that could either break wood or bust the lock. This was going to be a problem because in prison, everything is locked away. This included the metal file cabinets, which all had steel bars placed down inside the handles and secured with another padlock so the file drawers could not be pulled open. Luckily, I found the one that was unlocked and quickly slid the long steel bar up and out.

Paul kept a lookout and kept motioning for me to hurry up. The steel bar was now in my hands and I tried to pry the lock and hasp from the wood, which didn't work. Realizing the limited time and the panic in Paul's eyes, I began beating the hell out of this box. After a few strikes, the heavy steel bar finally hit the wooden box at just the right angle and it fell apart. The wooden walls collapsed in on each other and the letters fell out like candy from a piñata.

Paul grabbed all the paperwork from the floor while I replaced the steel bar in the file cabinet handles. Together, we then went to the nearby bathroom and e ripped up each letter into tiny pieces and flushed all the evidence down the toilet.

We had to walk back past the mail boxes in order to get to our work location, and as we approached the area, we could hear the watch commander, who was now back in his office, saying rather loudly, "Jesus Christ, who the hell would break the mailboxes and leave them hanging like that from the wall?"

Then we heard Sergeant Farrell's distinctive Brooklyn voice telling the inquisitive lieutenant, "I don't know sir, maybe someone fell into the box and it broke apart? But you can be rest assured I will look into it."

Sergeant Farrell exited the watch commander's office and saw us down the hallway, waiting for the gate to open and allow us access to our work locations. He loudly approached us so that the Lieutenant could overhear him ask, "Did either of you two officers see what happened to the mailbox?"

In unison and shaking our heads we said, "No Sgt. Nothing." He winked and then said in a normal tone, "Guess you got the letters." That was the first of many times he saved us from getting into trouble.

C.O. Where's My Food?

In the reception blocks everything used to be run very much like military boot camp. All the inmates are required to be fully dressed and standing in at their cell doors with the light on for the 7:00am count. This is a mandatory standing count. It's in the rule book that each inmate signs for and it is thoroughly explained in the block orientation on their first day. The midnight officer wakes each inmate at 6:30am and tells him to get dressed and ready for the 7:00am count.

So when I or anyone else comes on duty, the first thing I yell out loudly over the loudspeaker system is, "On the count." There is to be no talking as I walk from cell to cell and make sure they are each alive, fully dressed, and ready for all routine movement. As I mentioned earlier, in reception the inmates have scheduled tests and examinations each and every day that they must attend and complete.

At 7:05 am, I would clear the count. This meant they could move away from the door and wait for the next routine call, which is breakfast.

At 7:20 a.m. or so, I would receive the call from my sergeant to bring the inmates to the mess hall. I would then go back to the loudspeaker and announce, "On the chow," as I opened each and every cell door from the control panel in front of me. The inmates would then line up in cell order and I would wait 30 seconds before my second and last announcement over the loudspeaker, "Last call on the chow." After the next 30 seconds I would lock all the doors from the control panel and go out and count the inmates to make sure I had all the inmates I was responsible for. During the early to mid-1980s each block had a second officer. The second officer was eliminated in the late 1980s because some administrator from Albany, who doesn't work in the prisons, said they were not necessary.

At this point, my partner would go from cell to cell to make sure each door was locked. This was done for two reasons: to check for inmates hiding in their cells and also to secure their cells so that other inmates do not go into another inmate's cell and take personal property.

While I'm done on the main part of the block and standing by the control panel, the inmates have lined up by me. You can see the intricate role that the second officer used to play. Many fights have taken place over stolen cigarettes or photos of inmates loved ones when one inmate would dart into the cell of another inmate while the block officer is monitoring another area the block.

On one particular day, I was supposed to have 36 inmates, but I counted only 35. My partner, who was my senior, hollered to me that one inmate was still in his cell. The inmate was now shaking his door, trying to come out and yelling, "C.O., my door."

To make a point, especially in a reception unit, I replied with, "Too late for breakfast. You were dressed and ready fifteen minutes ago for the count and you heard 35 other cells slam shut." I then gave the go ahead for the 35 inmates who obeyed the rules to exit the block towards the outside courtyard.

But this guy kept shouting, "C.O., my breakfast," and I answered with, "Maybe at lunch you will move a little faster."

Once we were at the mess hall each officer has to give the area sergeant the total number of inmates we brought down to be fed.

"How many you got, Leo?"

"I have 35, Sarge. One took too long."

"Okay, bring him a tray back," he said. The sergeant was going through the motions of having the inmate fed so that we wouldn't have to do any paperwork and the imprudence of a misbehavior report. Sometimes there is an inmate who will approach you prior to the morning meal and let you know he is not feeling well or that he is not going to be finished using the lavatory in time. In those cases we would use common sense and bring back a Styrofoam tray with the meal in it for them, via the block porter.

After that meal we returned to the block and locked the 35 men in their cells. The inmate who missed breakfast was still yelling and insisting that he get his breakfast. We probably would have given it to him, but his demanding attitude negated any leniency in my mind. Also, the other inmates would have seen this and realized that they too could lag behind whenever they wanted and a meal would be brought to them like room service.

The tray that the porter carried back was placed in the officers' station and the senior officer was waving me back up the stairs and towards him.

"What's his problem?" he asked.

"He wants his meal," I answered.

"He's still whining about that? Fuck him."

And that was the end of that. We ended up using the sugar packets from the feed up tray for our own coffee and we spilt the toast.

But that wasn't the end of it. "C.O." said the block porter. "Seventeen wants to talk to of you about his breakfast."

The senior officer looked at me and said, "Leo, go down to his cell and tell him if he keeps up that noise, he will miss lunch also."

I walked down the stairs and approached his cell again and in his heavy accent, he said, "My food?"

As I was again explaining that he missed his meal because he didn't exit his cell when he was ordered to do so, he did something extremely unexpected, something I had never seen before and never saw again in my 25- year career. The inmate backed away from his cell door so he was in my full view, and took a sharpened pen from his pocket, and quickly plunged the pen into his neck. As blood began to spurt from his neck, the reality of what he just did sunk in. The blood had started to flow from all around the pen wound and was now squirting from his neck. He fell onto his bed and within a few short seconds the white sheet on his bed had turned a reddish brown. Having never experienced anything like this and without wanting to yell and alarm everyone, I ran up the stairs into the control booth and told the senior officer. He made a quick phone call and we both went down to the inmate's cell for another look.

We both looked at the inmate, and he didn't move at all.

The medical team arrived within minutes, along with the area sergeant, and quickly began emergency treatment. While they were busy attending to the bleeding inmate and everyone's attention was drawn inside the cell, the senior officer handed me the Styrofoam tray, which now had the emptied sugar packets and remnants of eaten toast in it, and said, "Go put this tray by the door."

Making sure no one saw me, I put the tray at the base of the cell by the door. This is where the inmates traditionally placed their finished feed-up trays. They would slide it out on the floor and under their door so that the inmate porter could easily pick it up and throw it away.

The medical team eventually stabilized the inmate and secured him on the stretcher. We then had a few volunteer inmates carry the inmate to the hospital. It was then that the sergeant asked me what happened.

Realizing that the inmate might eventually mention something about the food, I pointed to the tray and said, "I couldn't fully make out his broken English, but I think he was angry over the cold food in his tray." I then bent down to open the tray to "investigate" in front of him and remarked, "Looks like he ate most of it though."

"Ok, make sure you put that in your report," he said as he walked away.

I Stubbed My Toe

One of my duties over the years included being a "red-dot" officer, which is a person who responds immediately to any and all incidents within the prison. On the day shift there are only five of us red dots scattered around the facility. New York State Department of Corrections refuses to staff response teams on standby like you see in movies or TV shows. In many instances, the administration will not even fill red-dot posts, or they cleverly reassign the officer as a way to avoid hiring overtime. On their planning charts that are submitted to Albany headquarters, it will appear as if these red-dot positions are being filled, but they in fact are not.

Consequently, many times when you respond to a red-dot call, you are expecting help which may not arrive. There are other times when the officers, who are not red dots, leave their posts against the rules in order to help a brother officer. They realize that they may be brought up on departmental disciplinary charges, but in prison, the only ones we can rely on are our brother and sister officers.

One particular red-dot alarm came over the radio from Central Headquarters (CHQ) for response to housing unit 2D, which was located less than 50 yards from my primary work location. A good friend of mine at the time, Rich Connolly, who was one of the best officers I have ever worked with, happened to be talking to me in my area when we heard the red-dot call. The idea of the red-dot response is to prevent us from all running directly into a trap if the inmates intentionally stage a fight or incident in one part of the prison as a ruse. If we all responded to the fake fight, then the inmates could possibly take over the other part of the prison.

Right after we heard the call, Officer Connolly and I ran up the two flights of concrete stairs and into 2D block. Upon running through the front door on the television area, we immediately observed one inmate with a sharpened weapon attacking another inmate. The other 30 or so inmates in the immediate area had formed a circle and were watching but not involved. The inmate who was being attacked was using a chair, trying to fend off his attacker just like a lion tamer. The aggressor continued to attack in a slashing motion and was met with a thrusting chair.

The clanging of our keys and commotion on the radio caused the observing inmates to move quickly out of our way. Simply because of the way we ran into the block, I was closer to the aggressor and Connolly was closer to the inmate with the chair. Obviously, the inmate protecting himself was not going to put the chair down until the inmate trying to stab him was subdued and the weapon was secured.

In those few seconds I moved to within arms reach of the inmate with the weapon, which I now saw was a razor blade attached to a toothbrush. I ordered him to drop the weapon and could see in his eyes that he was in a zone of pure aggression. He was not listening to anything anyone was saying. All he wanted to do was stab the other inmate.

As he lunged at the other inmate who was now behind me, I grabbed the wrist that was holding the weapon. Simultaneously, I applied an aikido move that put him in such pain that he dropped the weapon about a second before I slammed him into the wall and then drove his whole body to the floor. The other inmates were just watching, but we still had to make sure that none of them grabbed the weapon, which was now on the concrete floor of the block.

Connolly had secured the other inmate by this time as well, so this whole incident took about one minute in time. I now had the aggressor on the floor with both arms behind his back in what we call a "come-a-long" technique, which is also rooted in Aikido. It creates pain in the wrist of the inmate by manipulating the bones and tendons against each other as it allows the officer to maintain control of the inmate without the use of mechanical restraints. If he resists, he hurts himself. It's only a temporary measure so you still need handcuffs eventually.

Having both inmates under control and making sure the weapon was out of his reach, I keyed my radio and calmly transmitted, "Cancel red-dot. Situation is under control. Anyone responding please bring handcuffs with them. I repeat, I need one pair of handcuffs and situation is under control." This transmission let any officer responding recognize that they needn't run and take the chance of injuring themselves on the way to assisting the situation.

A short time later another officer arrived and handed me handcuffs and I applied the mechanical restraints. The area supervisor had arrived sometime during the commotion and commended Connolly and me on a job well done, and asked us if we had any injuries. Richie and I looked at each other and both shook our heads no. We had secured two fighting inmates, one with a weapon, and neither of us was hurt. But that's not the way it usually happens.

After any incident, DOCS requires mounds and mounds of paperwork. Our few seconds of response will now be analyzed for months by administrators and the inspector general officers in Albany headquarters. IG officers are typically just a bunch of "want to be cops" who are afraid to work in the prison.

After this incident, Connolly and I brought both inmates to the hospital to have them seen by medical staff and then we filled out all of our reports.

About an hour later we handed our stack of "wasted paper" to our sergeant and he said, "I thought the two of you said neither of you were injured."

We again surprisingly looked at each other and replied, "We're not."

"Well, the watch commander called me and said one officer was going home injured from that incident or 'use of force.'"

"Sarge, neither of us is hurt" I said.

Frustrated, he picked up the phone and called the watch commander. "Lieutenant, I have both Leo and Connolly in front of me and neither of them are hurt and they were the only two involved in the use of force."

He went on to say, "Neither of the inmates is complaining of injuries either." As he listened, he looked at us as shook his head in a manner of disgust. "Oh, I see. Okay. Thank you." He hung up the phone with a loud bang.

"You'll never believe this one," he said, still shaking his head. "While you two were up on 2D rolling around with two inmates and a razor blade, the officer in the tunnel got hurt and she's the one going on out on workers compensation with an injury."

Richie and I looked at each other and couldn't figure out how that was even possible, and our amazement quickly turned to anger as we heard the whole story.

The officer who works in the tunnel control booth controls all movement into and out of the complex where we worked and where the red-dot incident took place. When the tunnel officer heard me say, over the radio, that I needed handcuffs, she "quickly" handed a pair to a responding officer who was running through the tunnel area. She claims that in her haste to pass the handcuffs to the responding officer as quickly as possible, she stubbed her toe against a wall in the tunnel control booth. I guess she didn't hear the part when I said the situation was under control. We laughed about this at first, but it was sickening that she eventually received a permanent disability for that bullshit injury.

Where Did That Razor Blade Come From?

One quiet day, my area supervisor called me and asked me to come to his office as soon as I could. I entered casually, saying, "What's up Sarge?"

"Leo, we have an inmate on B-Block who has been giving a female officer a hard time and making lewd comments. He's not doing anything that could get him locked up, but enough to undermine her control of the block. You and I are going to the block and you will pat down the inmate and find 'something' so that we can get him moved to the special housing unit (SHU)."

Knowing what he meant and acknowledging my upcoming task, I went to an inmate porter who I knew could get us a weapon. I told the inmate, "Bring me a shank, no questions asked."

Within minutes he returned and as he was talking to me, he dropped the weapon in a waste paper basket as he acted like he was adjusting his sneaker lace. He walked away and I picked up the weapon. In prison anything can be made into a weapon, and this was a razor blade that had been embedded into the plastic handle of a toothbrush. The inmates heat up and melt the plastic until it's sticky and can be molded. The razor is then pushed into the hot mushy plastic until it hardens. The razor is now affixed and ready to do some serious damage.

I'm asked by the public over and over, "Where do they get the razor blades?" Every inmate is allowed to buy razor blades from the prison commissary or prison store. They buy the packs of ten disposable razors and then make a weapon or two for their safety or to carry out a hit. They use the other ones to shave.

I put the weapon in my pocket and the Sergeant and I walked up to the block where the problem inmate was still yelling obscenities from his cell. The inmate could have been written up for his behavior, but that takes days for a hearing and the problem needed to be addressed immediately. When you have one inmate challenging the authority of the block officer, the situation has to be dealt with swiftly.

The sergeant and I approached the problem child's cell and when the sergeant signaled for the block officer to unlock it, the loud click of the electronic lock got his attention.

"What's up C.O.? What's going on? I didn't do nuffin," he said, not getting up off his bed.

I ordered him to exit his cell with his hands behind his back. Otherwise, it would be considered a hostile action and he would be taken out of his cell forcefully. Now dealing with a male C.O., his demeanor was quite different. He said, "No problem C.O. You got that," and exited his cell just as we had asked, with his hands behind his back.

I then told him to place both of his hands on the wall in order to be patted down. He complied and was very polite with me and the Sergeant. I didn't know this guy's background or home life. Maybe he had issues with females. But what I did know was that he was a potential security problem and he needed to be promptly removed from that block.

Right before I began my pat frisk, I reached into my pocket and removed "his" weapon. As my hands moved down towards his waste and into his pockets, I told the Sergeant, "We got something here. It's a weapon."

The Sergeant removed his handcuffs from the pouch on his belt and told the inmate he would be handcuffed and moved to the SHU

"Yo, that's fucked up C.O. You know that's not mine."

"It is now," I replied.

He smiled because he knew the game. "You got that C.O., but it's still fucked up."

As we escorted him to the SHU, he kept telling us that we could have settled this in a different way. "Why don't you just let me and that female C.O. settle this problem ourselves?"

"That's exactly why you are being moved," the Sergeant stated. He went on to tell the inmate, "You want to be a tough guy with the female officers? Now you can be a tough guy with the other tough guys in the SHU."

Here's the amazing part: We entered the many secured doors and gates of the SHU, to the place where the SHU officers take control of the inmate. Each inmate entering the SHU is escorted to the strip frisk room. The inmate, via commands of the two or more male correction officers, will remove each article of clothing. The SHU sergeant always monitors this process. Then a strip frisk and body cavity search is conducted on the now naked inmate to make sure he has nothing secreted in his body cavities upon entering the SHU. The SHU houses the worst of the worst and the last thing they need are weapons smuggled in.

I was in the control booth filling out paperwork for his admission when the Sergeant came in and said with a smile, "Leo, come here. You won't believe this one."

By this time I had been in the department for about 15 years and had about one-hundred of use-of-force incidents in my career and thousands of strip frisks, but had never had this happen before. As the SHU officers were performing the admission strip frisk, they had the inmate bend over at his waist and spread the cheeks of his rear end. Trust me when I tell you, we don't enjoy performing strip frisks either, but it has to be done. When this inmate spread his cheeks, the officer noticed a string hanging from his anal cavity.

The inmate was told that he could remove the string item in his rear end on his own or he could be brought to the hospital and have a doctor remove whatever it was attached to the string. After a moment, he slowly tugged on the string and dropped the item on the floor.

He was ordered not to move as the officer, using latex gloves, retrieved the yet unidentified item, which after carefully unwrapping its protective cover, turned out to be a razor blade. It was carefully wrapped in tape over a matchbook cover to protect the inmate from the sharp edge of the blade. It had been covered in Vaseline before being inserted into his anus.

I stood at the doorway and when he saw me, he smiled and shrugged his shoulders. I said, "Try telling them the other weapon wasn't yours at the hearing."

He smiled and said, "You got that right."

The inmate ultimately made a deal at his hearing to plead guilty to one weapon charge and the other weapon charge would be dismissed altogether. He knew there was no way he could claim that someone placed a weapon up his rear end.

We killed two birds with one stone that day. His hatred towards women correction officers was now halted and on record by being locked in the SHU. So we took a potential problem off the block and we also got two weapons that we would have never found. Who knows—maybe he was going to use it on the female officer.

I Memorized It

One of my most entertaining memories took place at Elmira prison in the late 1980s. Elmira is a very old and historic boy's reformatory that was turned into a prison. It looks very much like a red brick castle brought from England or Scotland and gently placed on a steep hill in Elmira, New York. As you travel on Route 17 (now I-86) on a clear day, you can see the prison from the highway.

Being deeply rooted with history and traditions, the prison had its own way of doing things, and during this time in corrections, there was a concerted effort to have more minorities become supervisors. Once you pass a civil service exam in New York, you work wherever the next opening is anywhere in the state.

From that exam in 1989, there were five black sergeants sent to Elmira prison from other prisons in the New York City and Hudson Valley area. To put this in perspective, when I worked at Elmira, there was only one black officer and three Hispanic officers in the whole prison. Now there were going to be five black sergeants. Having been from the Hudson Valley my whole life and working in both Green Haven and Downstate prisons for almost eight years before transferring to Elmira, I knew three of the five newly promoted black sergeants very well.

The administration knew full well that these black sergeants were not going to stay at Elmira for the rest of their careers, and for the most part they would only be there a matter of months until they could transfer and be reassigned to a facility closer to their homes. In the meantime, management at Elmira started enforcing directives using these new sergeants. Since the new sergeants were on probation for one year, they had to do whatever they are ordered to do or they would lose their stripes and go back to being a correction officer.

With this being the case, the new black sergeants were ordered to start enforcing the directive that covered "Roll Call" or line-up for each shift. Whereas the officers were used to sitting at tables, drinking coffee and saying "here" when their name was called, the directive insisted that the officers be standing and at attention in formal lines from this point forward. If you are an officer and get promoted to sergeant at your own prison, it is more difficult for you to order people who were your equal co-workers and friends to do something that you yourself were doing a few days ago. So the genius of this plan was to have the new black sergeants whip everyone into shape before they left and then have those directives maintained by the permanent sergeants thereafter.

As you can imagine, during this period there were a lot of problems and racial statements made, and the funniest was when a good friend of mine from

Downstate was with one of the new black sergeants. After a few weeks the full compliance with standing at roll call was completed. Now that the officers were standing in lines, the next hurdle was to have each officer wear a nametag and their collar brass insignia or whatever else was missing from their uniforms.

The Sergeant in charge, Sgt. Benson, appeared that day and walked up and down the ranks of officers with his notebook out and pen in hand. He was short in stature and when he made his visual inspection of the officers, his eye line was directly to most of the officer's chests. So he stared right at the nametag area and moved quickly up and down the lines as the Chart-Sergeant called off the names from the podium at the front of the room.

In between the responses of "here" or "present," you could overhear any of the sergeants asking the officers things like, "Why aren't your shoes shined? When is the last time you had a hair cut? Why is your t-shirt blue instead of white? Where is your tie? Are those department issued pants? "Why isn't your shirt tucked in properly?" And so on.

But the most famous answer during line-up was about to be given to Sgt. Benson. Only looking up enough for a quick glance to see if the officer he was now in front of was in compliance with the uniform directive, Benson noticed a missing nametag. A missing nametag to a supervisor is equivalent to a police officer finding a pound of drugs.

Benson stopped and looked up at the officer's face and asked, "Where is your nametag, officer?"

I was two officers from the right and watched out of the corner of my eye as the much larger and taller white officer responded with a slight hesitation. He motioned for Benson to lean in towards him as if he was going to whisper an intimate secret. With pen to notebook Benson took the bait and leaned in. "They told me my name at the academy. I memorized it and then threw the nametag away."

Everyone in close proximity broke out in laughter. Even Benson, being a much more experienced officer, realized this was not the time to do battle and laughed along saying, "Okay, okay, that was a good one, but tomorrow, go through the garbage, find it, and wear it." It was a common sense way for a supervisor to make a point and not escalate something minor.

All of these black sergeants quickly transferred back to their regular facilities.

Learning a Lesson the Hard Way

When a red-dot response is called, that means that a fellow officer is in trouble and needs help now. In some parts of the prison, it could take up to five minutes for us to arrive at a red-dot location, and you can imagine how out of breath even the most athletic person would be once they finally arrived. Consequently, when help arrives, they're not much assistance at that point. For that reason, it's expected that if you are nearby and can help, you do help. It's bad enough that we are already greatly out numbered and understaffed.

On average, a correction officer in New York State prison watches 60 inmates by him or herself. What the public does not realize is that in New York State the maximum security inmates are out of their cells from seven in the morning until 10 or 11 at night each and every day. Inmates are generally locked in their cells only for counts and to sleep. During the day, they are participating in trade school, at work, at the gym, at recreation, in barber shop, the library, the law library, the yard, etc. Of course, the disciplinary inmates do not fall into this category.

Of the 60,000 inmates in New York State, 30,000 of the state's medium security inmates are never locked up and the other 30,000 are only locked in for about eight hours a day. The medium security inmates are housed in dorms that are designed like college dorms with each bed separated only by a half wall that would remind you of a secretary's cubicle. The scary part about the medium security prisons is that many of the inmates are actually maximum security inmates that have murdered, raped and robbed. Since the maximum security prisons are so overcrowded, the Department of Corrections waves their magic wand, relaxes the criteria, and makes a maximum security inmate into a medium security inmate. And you can imagine the trouble they cause within the medium prisons.

Each evening in these dorms, when the lights go out, there is only one Correction Officer is assigned to watch 60 inmates, many of whom are maximum security inmates. There are many instances of officers being hit with flying bars of soap once the lights go out, and the inmates know there is nothing that can be done about it.

Currently in 2009, the maximum security prisons in New York State are operating at around124% capacity, the medium prisons are 96% capacity, and the minimums are at 61% for an overall operating capacity of approximately 102%. Correction officers are outnumbered and the prisons are understaffed so when help is needed, you better get there and get there quickly.

Many years when ago a red-dot alert blurted over the radio, the few of us who were in the area, grabbing a quick coffee, dropped everything and responded.

We got the situation under control, and when we returned to get our coffee cups, we realized this one piece-of-shit officer never even moved from his chair and was still eating his donut. We rightfully got angry.

"Hey, asshole, where were you during the red-dot call?" I asked.

"I figured you guys had enough help so I stayed here to watch the coffee."

His failure at comedy only infuriated us. There are only two reasons not to help a fellow officer, fear and laziness. We had known this particular officer for many years now and he didn't respond for both reasons. He was beyond lazy and definitely afraid of the inmates. We also knew that as an escort officer he was famous for taking a nap in the back storage room whenever he could.

So we waited until the next time that he was "taking a break" and decided he needed to learn his lesson. Years before, he would have met with "parking lot" justice, but since the time of honor among officers had passed, we had to resort to something else. Nowadays, most people cry to the administration that another officer is threatening them or has challenged them to the parking lot, taking peer pressure out of the box as an effective tool.

On this day, we observed the sleeping piece of crap comfortably lounging on an old barber chair, with no sign of regret from his earlier lack of courage. Even in his dreams he was not struggling with his conscious decision not to come to the aid of a fellow officer. So we took an old inmate's blanket from the dirty laundry pile on the floor of the storage room and firmly placed it over his head and held it there. It took him a second or two to wake up, but it was too late. Between fists and bars of soap, we pounded his face and body so rapidly that when he slid from the chair to the floor he landed face first. We quickly left the room and scattered to our assigned areas and back to our normal routines.

By later in the day, I had actually forgotten about the "lesson" altogether, until we were waiting at the time clock around 3:00pm. That's when I heard other officers making comments about this officer and the condition of his face. Trying not to seem over eager, I stretched my neck to see the results of the "blanket party." His right eye had grown to three times its normal size and was very dark and was nearly closed. This officer was in a difficult position because he couldn't say he was sleeping when he got roughed up. The question would be asked, "Who did this? Was it officer or inmate?" Then the question would be, "Why?" He would then have to answer, "Because I'm a lazy, scared piece of shit."

Those questions would be asked by him each every time for the next week or so whenever he had to look himself in the mirror. Deep down, he already knew the answer to these questions. We just made him more aware of them.

Son, Are You Hearing Me?

One red-dot call that I responded to took place in a courtyard, where two passing housing units began a large scale brawl. One group of 36 inmates was returning from the mess hall and entering their housing unit while the other group of 36 inmates was exiting their housing unit on their way to the mess hall. By the time I arrived, there had already been a few inmates who had had their faces sliced open with razor blades and a few others scrambling looking for something to protect themselves with. The inmates that did not want to be involved stayed up against the wall so their non-involvement would be evident.

The first thing I noticed was all the blood on the concrete and then I saw the inmates holding their faces in an attempt to stop the spurting blood. Some had taken off their shirts to apply pressure to their wounds. One thing about prison, the primal instincts of survival come back to us very quickly. All rules are forgotten when it comes to protecting one's life.

When enough officers finally arrived, we began to break up the fights. We entered the war zone and I began to pull one inmate off of another, and with all this punching and hitting still going on, I didn't see that one of the inmates had a razor blade tightly gripped in his punching hand. I had to go swiftly from the pulling motion of his arm to a punching motion to his face to make him drop the weapon. I remember that he was in such a zone that I had to punch him in the face many times before he finally fell off of the inmate he was attacking. When he finally released the razor from his grasp, it fell to the ground right into a pool of blood.

I began the process of dragging him off the other inmate and away from the weapon, but he attempted to get back on his feet. He was much larger than me, so the last thing I wanted was to have this guy up on his feet and going after that weapon. It took way to much effort to make him drop it in the first place. So to get control of him, I grabbed his wrist and elbow and went to flip him on his back. This technique created so much pain that the inmate actually assisted me in hoisting him into the air and away from the pain. But as the inmate was flying through the air, he used his foot to kick another officer who was in close proximity and trying to subdue another inmate. I felt the kick was intentional and recorded it in the report I later submitted.

Once I had the inmate back on the ground, I used my foot to apply pressure to the back of his neck. My foot grinding his face firmly against the concrete ground of the courtyard was enough for him to finally just lay there and survey the carnage from a defeated angle. He could see that all the fighting had been halted and their battle was over for that day.

Once this bloody mess was cleaned up, every officer and inmate had to go to the hospital and be checked for injuries. Then we wrote our reports and changed our bloodied uniforms. It had been quite a day.

About a week later I was in the training trailer, teaching, ironically, the "use of force" course to other officers when I received a phone call saying that the captain wanted to see me. I explained that I was in the middle of a training class and was told to report during my next break.

When we broke for lunch, I walked up to the main building to see what the captain needed. This was a captain who I had never personally dealt with before since he had transferred in from Fishkill prison only about six months prior. He was older man with white hair and close to retirement age.

"Son," he said, waving me in. "Take a seat."

I thought back to my last meeting with a captain, now about 15 years before, and thought, do they send these guys to some school where they all learn to call all officers "son?" Anyway, I thought he had called me up to his office for something concerning the training curriculum I was teaching, but he went on to ask me about the report I wrote on the courtyard fight. The part of the report in question was where I had written that I observed the inmate kick the officer.

"In your report you say he intentionally kicked the other officer," the Captain said. "How can you be so sure it was intentional?"

"Sir, in my opinion the inmate made an intentional motion with his leg to kick the other officer while he was in the air," I said.

The Captain then went into this long diatribe about how sometimes things don't actually happen the way we think we see things happen. "Son, would you be willing to change your report to say that the other officer was 'accidentally' kicked?"   "Sir, If you are ordering me to change my report and reflect that, then I will follow the direct order."

His face turned red and if he was about 30 years younger, he probably would have wanted to quickly make this a physical conversation. The key part to keep in mind is that DOCS does not like to report problems or record them on paper. If an officer does something, they are all about reporting, but when it comes to assaults or unusual incidents, they like to keep it quiet. So when something like this incident happens, the captain is contacted by some administrator in Albany and he is told to see if they can get this assault erased or at least watered down. This way, when DOCS issues reports to the public or the press concerning violence in New York State prisons, it will appear that violence and violent incidents are down.

So now you know a well kept secret.

"Son, are you listening to me," the Captain continued. "It's possible that the inmate accidentally brushed against the officer as you threw him to the ground."

One of the courses I taught to other officers was report writing. We had noticed this trend of asking officers to change their reports as a way to underreport incidents and thus make the department look like everything was running well with less security staff. I, for one, was not going to fall for this farce and repeated, "Sir, if you want me to change the report, I will reflect that in my second report. Otherwise my report stands the way I wrote it."

He knew I was right and deep down he was probably sickened by what he was being told to do by some guy in a suit who had never even seen an inmate in his life. He was probably also saddened by what the department had become. He knew my second report would read, "On direct order from Captain 'Gutless,' I am changing this report to say the inmate accidentally kicked the officer," or something like that.

But the Captain was stubborn, and not giving up. He droned on with this story about how when he was a young officer, making rounds one day outside a housing a unit, someone dumped a bucket of water from a window above and soaked him. He immediately ran up to the tier and found the inmate porter with the empty bucket and started yelling at him. As the water dripped from his hair and down onto his uniform, the porter explained that he dumps the water every day from the window, but that it was not intentional.

"Son, are you listening me. It's possible that it was an accident."

He almost had me with that sappy story, but all I could hear over and over was "son."

"Sir, no disrespect intended," I replied, but I don't feel comfortable changing my report and I think the hearing officer should make that decision based on all the evidence. By the way, maybe that inmate dumped the water on your head many years ago and lied to you and he did it on purpose."

He shook his head in disgust. "You're dismissed."

I walked out of the office and heard him pick up his phone. So I took a slow drink of water from the water fountain directly outside his door and listened. I heard him say, "No sir, he's not going to change it so I guess we will have to report it to Albany." That meant he was talking to someone higher up than him because he called him sir, and they were holding off on reporting the assault altogether, as I had suspected.

The inmate was eventually found not guilty by the hearing officer for the additional assault charge on the officer, but he was found guilty of assaulting an inmate with a weapon and sent to the disciplinary special housing unit.

Dirty Little Secret

The New York State Department of Corrections manipulates data and underreports incidents on a regular basis, and one of the most underreported items is the presence contraband. Each day, the housing unit or block officer is responsible to conduct three cell or cube searches in his area. But the job of a correction officer has become quite burdensome with paperwork over the years, which makes almost impossible to do anything other than paperwork, let alone conduct thorough searches of three cells each day.

When I began my career we had two documents we had to fill out—count slips and cell searches. Today, there are now so many reports that they actually have officers counting soap balls and measuring the contents of Ajax cans. God forbid you are off by one soap ball when they come around and check. It's almost as bad as having an inmate escape. Not as bad, but almost.

The number of forms and documents that must be completed signed and turned in to your supervisor by the afternoon count each day is the true definition of repetitiveness for the sake of creating a paper trail. By the time we complete the breakfast run, it's approximately 9:00am and we start the "callouts," which consists of sending inmates to different areas of the facility for miscellaneous reasons. Some are going to see the counselor, others to sick call, the law library, gym, work, school, etc. Passes have to written for each inmate, or in some cases, escort officers have to be called. Some inmates are returning from their callouts before you even finished sending inmates out and completing the passes. Plus, we have phone calls, inmates who are staying on the block and need items, and a dozen other distractions.

With limited officers, daily closing of security posts, and the administrators in Albany hindering overtime in order to maintain their high salaries, we simply cannot accomplish our jobs. So here is another dirty little secret. Most of the time we can't and don't do cell searches. Since the act of completing the cell search form has become more important than actually doing the cell search, many of us have resorted to completing the form without ever stepping into the cell. The form is marked, " NCF," which means, "No Contraband Found." And if you dare say you didn't have the time or opportunity to do the cell searches, you will have a bigger headache than you would get from just filling out the form as if you had done the searches.

So on paper it appears that there is less contraband in the prisons. In reality there is currently probably more contraband in New York State prisons than there has ever been. That's why whenever you read in the local paper about a prison being locked down for a major disturbance; we find truckloads of weapons and contraband. It's not that all of a sudden this contraband appeared out of nowhere. It's been there for years, but we haven't had the manpower to effectively and properly search the prison. During a lockdown, when the inmates are all locked in their cells, we have time to thoroughly search them because the administration in Albany will authorize the hiring of security overtime and staff the prison the way it should be staffed on a daily basis. The public will read about all the weapons found during the lockdown and think the inmates were preparing for World War III based on the amount of contraband found. Reality is, this stuff is there all the time and the inmates are prepared every day, but we don't have the manpower to search.

All Hell Broke Loose

On a few occasions I had the "privilege" of being doused with a concoction that only the most savage and rudimentary mind could think of. I say privilege only because when this occurs, it means you are doing your job and we can consider it a badge of honor. How else can we rationalize the disgusting thing that just happened to us?

The primitive inmate intellect is typically quite simple yet surprisingly effective. Their actions are very similar to other animals who toss their feces at each other during an aggressive outbreak. They learn how to survive and the inmates would have done quite well in the caveman era. So even though it's a disgusting custom of inmates and animals alike, it is explainable. Unfortunately at times, officers have to lower themselves to this same level in order for the prisoner intellect to understand.

The ingredient of this inmate brew is normally water, urine and feces. They will allow the liquid to ferment in a cup for a few days. They do this so that the stench gets to the point that any normal civilized person will immediately start gagging upon contact. Sometimes, they will add cheap tobacco to the mix, which helps the liquid stench stick to the intended target. You will now have a fragrance attached to you that even tomato juice cannot even get rid of.

There were a few times, while working at the Special Housing Unit (SHU) in Elmira, where all hell broke loose. There is no rhyme or reason for the outbursts and they are quite erratic in nature.

On this particular day, we had a large group of inmates who were already being penalized for throwing feces or "dousing" officers. These inmates had since been placed in cells with plexiglass mounted to the bars of their cell. In theory, this would prevent the inmates from further throwing their feces out of their cells. This was supposed to halt the feces from exiting the cell when thrown so that it would bounce back into their own cell, but the inmates will always find a way.

On the July day I'm recalling, those inmates behind the plexiglass had realized the framing that secured the plexiglass to their bars was made from wood. So they pushed flammable items under their cell bars, and in concert, ignited some paper products and blankets to the point that the wood and plastic were now in a roaring blaze.

Thick black smoke quickly filled the area of these cells, toward the back of the tier. The sergeant on duty, who was new, ran down the tier and began opening the windows. What he didn't realize is that there were blower fans mounted in the ceilings precisely for situations like this. His opening of the windows prevented the fans from working at all. The billowing smoke got worse and we decided we had to go back down the tier and close and re-secure the opened windows so that the ventilators could do their job.

Now, with smoke as their cover, the inmates pelted us with cups and cups of the "concoction." Three other officers and I closed windows, turning our backs to the throwing inmates to protect us from getting feces in our mouths and eyes, but also to take gasps of fresh air from the windows that we were closing. The smell of the feces stuck to our clothing and between that awful stench and the thick smoke, we could barley breathe.

Once the windows were finally closed and the fans began to work properly, the smoke started to clear. The inmates were all standing at their cells smiling like little kids who had just gotten caught stealing a cookie from the cupboard. The fires were still burning on the cells that had the plexiglass shields, and other spots burned in front of other cells, where blankets, books and other objects had been thrown to feed the fires.

A Lieutenant then arrived on the scene. He was an old school Lieutenant who didn't take any crap from anyone—no pun intended. He had a raincoat on, which protected him from the cup of feces that was just leaving cell 54. Cell 54 was the last cell on the tier and in the SHU, so the smoke was just clearing as the inmate figured he would get one last throw in before we could see clearly where it came from. But he didn't see the Lt. had come from the other side of the tier, and he hit him dead center on his raincoat in the chest area.

The stoic Lieutenant did not panic and he didn't look for cover. He looked right at the inmate with a grin reminiscent of Clint Eastwood and said, "You are mine."

The tier looked a bomb had exploded. We later referred to it as "little Saigon." The brown fecal matter mixed with tobacco was clinging to the walls, windows and floors. Fires were still burning and the dripping plexiglass was creating an unbelievable amount of heat and smoke. The lingering smoke amplified the smell of the feces and we were all on the verge of throwing up. It was unbearable.

To put out the remaining fires, the Lieutenant unlocked the standpipe hose, which has to be completely and neatly unraveled for the water pressure to build up and for the hose to work properly. As we unraveled it, I grabbed the brass nozzle and took control of it. I couldn't wait to blast those yelling inmates away from their cells, especially the ones who were now freely throwing items from their cells because they knew we were back in control of the situation.

But once they realized we had the hose, they began to grab the mattress from their beds and hold them against the bars, as if they knew what was coming and had done this before.

I stood brazenly with the nozzle out in front of the cells, knowing that any minute a high-pressure hose would blast the inmates, the mattresses and anything else in the way of me and me "putting the fires out." A second officer came up behind me to help hold the hose in preparation of the strong surge of water. Then a third officer approached. The inmates peeked from behind their mattresses every few seconds waiting for the water.

Then I started yelling, "Where is the god-damn water?"

We could see them turning the spindle, releasing the water as fast as they could, and then we could hear it snaking through the hose. The inmates braced for the impact and just as we yelled to the inmates, "Get ready," as a way of saying, "Now it's your turn," the water dribbled out of the spout and dripped to the floor.

It was like Barney Fife in Mayberry and a bullet dropping from a revolver, and we just looked at each other and couldn't do anything but laugh. The inmates realized what was going on and they began to cackle. Knowing the hose was not working properly; the inmates lowered their mattresses and started throwing items again.

As we stood there, using the dribbling water to apply fresh water to our faces, it happened. The water began building and building to the point that it took the three of us to maintain it as it rushed out the nozzle of the hose. We blasted the fires, the cells, the mattresses and whatever else we could to show the inmates that this is what will happen each and every time they do something like this. You want a wet cell? You want a soaked mattress and soggy books? You want your legal work to be destroyed? Then go ahead and start another fire. We showed them!

The Lieutenant quickly and loudly pointed to the inmate who had earlier thrown the feces on him and said, "Knock that fucker down and soak his cell."

Obeying the Lieutenant we moved towards cell 54 and concentrated the rest of our efforts only on him. The inmate was clever, and hid behind the one part of his wall that we could not get to as we continued to drench his cell. We wanted to make sure his fire was out!

The Lieutenant then said, "Go around to the front of his cell and get that fucker."

So that's we did. We dragged the now very heavy and hard to control hose towards the front door of cell 54. The front doors of the cells were solid steel with two flaps on hinges. The flap toward the top portion of the door was an observation window that we could quickly unlatch and flip down to look in the cell to observe. The other flap was towards the bottom of each door where inmates would receive their three meals and mail.

We couldn't figure out where this guy was hiding in his cell, so like idiots, the two of us bent down to getter a better look through the lower metal flap, and he was there. We were both hit in the face with a cup full of liquid that burned our eyes to the point that we instinctively let go of the fire hose to rub our eyes. I don't know if you have ever had the pleasure of letting a fully pressurized fire hose go, but it's not recommended. Once we could both open our eyes again we saw a brass missile attached to a canvas hose darting all over the place and very near our heads. The inmate was in his cell laughing his ass off and yelling to the other inmates explaining what had happened with our hose. And to add to the confusion, they all started banging on their metal doors.

I finally grabbed the brass handle of the hose, which reminded me of a darting cobra, banging against the metal doors, the ceiling and the cinder block wall outside of cell 54. When we finally regained control of the hose, we used some of the water to irrigate our eyes and then proceeded to soak every bit of 54

cell. I will never forget that he was standing there with his mattress and laughing as

we fired the stream of water at him and his belongings. It had become a game to all

of us by that time and he acknowledged through his comments that he knew he had

gotten us and now it was time he got his. In a very weird way, the officers and the

inmates each earned more respect for one another that day and I personally was

never "doused" or "uzied" again in my career.

Drugs in Prison?

Many people ask how in the world the inmates get drugs in prison.

Admittedly, a small amount does come in through either civilian or security staff

and they are dealt with when caught. But the majority of drugs enter prisons

through packages or the visiting room.

Many inmates, especially those with drug money, pay friends and family members to hide drugs in various containers and then reseal them. With today's technology almost anyone, including the inmates friends and family members, can buy a "seal a meal" to hermetically reseal a plastic package of pepperoni or sandwich meat that is then sent to the inmate from a friend of family member from the outside. With the right resources and resolve, a can of coffee or tuna fish can be resealed. So that's one way drugs get in the prisons.

The most common way is from the visitors themselves. A female visitor comes to the prison with five or more balloons of heroin in her bra. She easily makes it through the metal detector because the drug-filled balloons don't have metal. Once she gets to the visiting room she goes into the bathroom and puts one of the balloons into her mouth. When she sees her husband or boyfriend she gives him a nice big kiss and the inmate swallows the balloon. She has all day to pass the other balloons because in many of New York's prisons, the visits last all day. It's not like you see on TV or in the movies where the inmates and visitors are communicating through a telephone or stopped from touching because of a piece of glass. That does not exist in New York. That is a myth that Hollywood continues to perpetrate on the public. In New York State, prisons visits are contact visits in which the inmates are touching and hugging throughout the day, which means they can kiss quite few times and pass the other balloons. You may be asking yourself, where is the security?

Well, one officer sits in the front of the visiting room and another is in the back, but he's busy frisking the incoming and exiting inmates. Let's say, for example, there are 50 inmates. That means there are at least 50 visitors. Some have children running around and others have both mothers and fathers visiting. You can easily have over a hundred people in the visiting room and probably a sexual incident going on somewhere in the room.

If you are an attentive officer, you'll notice that the inmate who is waiting for the drugs to be passed will wait until he knows the officer in the back is frisking an inmate. Once the inmate and visitor confirm the attention of the officer in the back of the room is drawn away, the inmate will have another inmate or visitor draw the attention of the officer in front so that the passing of drugs can be completed.

The rules that are specifically written for visitor's looks like a deterrent for this type of behavior, but carefully read rule number 8. This is the rule that is really enforced as a way to not enforce and negate rules 1-7.

RULES SPECIFIC TO THE VISITING ROOM

1. *Posted Rules: All inmates and visitors shall follow posted rules and directions of the visiting room officers. Allowable items may vary according to facility policy. No large bags or packages will be allowed in the visiting room. Lockers are available in the front gate area for such items.*
2. *Exchange: Visitors will not give anything to inmates, nor will inmates give anything to visitors, unless it is examined and approved by the officer.*
3. *Kissing: A visitor and inmate may embrace and kiss at the beginning and end of any contact visit. Brief kisses and embraces are also permitted during the course of the contact visit. However, prolonged kissing and what is commonly considered "necking" or "petting' is not permitted.*
4. *Hand Holding: A visitor and an inmate may hold hands as long as the hands are in plain view of others.*
5. *Seating: The officer in charge of the visiting room will make the seating arrangements. Seating arrangements will not be changed by the inmates or visitors.*
6. *Food: Only food and beverages purchased in the vending machines will be allowed in the visiting room, and only visitors are allowed to use the machines.*
7. *Pictures: Pictures of you and your loved one may be made available according to facility policy.*
8. *Visitor's Complaint: Visitors who wish to express a complaint against a staff member should request to see a security supervisor. Visitors who wish to lodge a complaint of unlawful discriminatory treatment shall send a written description outlining the particulars of the incident, including date, time, place, name(s) of person(s) involved, if known, and/or other documentation in support of the claim to:*

Director, Office of Diversity Management
New York State Department of Correctional Services
The Harriman State Campus - Building #2
1220 Washington Avenue
Albany, NY 12226-2050

See where the complaints go? Directly to Diversity management, and not security.

All inmates are stripped frisked after each visit, but nothing will be found. Two

days or so later, the balloon has finished its long trek down the excretory system

and exits in the privacy of the inmate's cell toilet. He now can begin dealing his drugs inside prison. You can't stop drugs in prison as long as there are packages and visits. Maybe they know that?

Do You Think This Is Wood?

One day when I was in my third year, my day was going along fine when two senior transportation officers entered my unit. When the transportation officers arrive, it's usually to take an inmate to court or a medical appointment. So I unlocked the door allowed them access into the block control panel. We chatted a bit because I knew one of the senior officers through his son, who was also a correction officer and was a very good friend of mine. We wrapped up the chat and they told me that they would signal me when they wanted the door unlocked of the inmate they were retrieving.

I watched them walk up the stairs and bang on the inmates door. I waited for their signal, but they just stood there talking to the inmate through the locked door. After a few minutes I realized there was a problem and that the inmate was refusing to go along with them. For various reasons, many inmates refuse to leave their cells when they are ordered to do so and this was one of those times. Some don't want to go to court and some just want to be left alone. I watched them maintain a conversation with the inmate and decided to call the senior officer's son as a way to bust chops.

"George," I said, "your dad and his partner are on my block and they are having a tough time getting an inmate to exit his cell." When I called him I had no idea that he would magically appear on my block, but George was George. He was about six foot and not an ounce of fat on him. All he used to do was work out and was very proud of his bulging biceps and triceps. I don't recall how this started, but he used to make a muscle and point to the mountain of solid skin and say, "What do think, this is wood?" It was just something stupid that a 21 year old used to say and it was quite comical the way he said it.

"Is my old man still up there talking to the inmate?" he asked when he arrived.

I pointed in their direction and said, "See for yourself."

His father saw him as I pointed and he shrugged his shoulders indicating that they were getting nowhere.

As George left my control console, he muttered, "Let me go show those old timer's how to get an inmate out of the cell."

I watched as he cockily sprinted up the stairs and proudly smiled as he approached his dad and the other senior officer. His father had about 20 years as a correction officer at the time and George and I had three, but George was going to show them how it's done. That was George. Collectively, they signaled for me to open the cell door and I saw George enter and then saw his father and his partner go in.

About 20 seconds later, the older officers walked out with the inmate in handcuffs, but they were all laughing—including the inmate. Then George came out holding his nose. As the story goes, George walked in and the inmate backed up, and put his hands up and said, "I ain't going nowhere."

Showing off in front of his dad and the other old-timer, George flexed his arm and made a muscle. He pointed with his other hand and said, "What do think, this is wood?" I guess he figured the inmate would just be intimated by his size and would give up peacefully. Wrong.

As George was saying the word "wood," the inmate punched him in the face. The three of them quickly pounced on the inmate and got their shots in as they placed handcuffs on him. Everything happened so quickly that they were still laughing as they escorted the inmate out of the block. When George came back down to my control consol and told me the story, I laughed as well.

George took it in stride, but was very embarrassed, and to make it worse, any time the three of us were together, his dad would make an old man's muscle and jokingly say, "What do you think this is, wood? Bam!" and laugh.

Going on Vacation

"Leo, the Captain said I have to give you a verbal reprimand for eating toast," the Sergeant said one day.

I smiled thinking he was joking with me, but soon realized he was serious. "What toast?"

"The Captain said he had just made rounds in your area and could see you down the hallway eating the state's toast."

"Sarge, how many years have you seen me walk up to the cafeteria and buy my toast?"

He nodded almost in embarrassment that he had to deal with such silly matters. At Downstate prison we have a small cafeteria where we can purchase breakfast and lunch. Not all prisons have these, but I took advantage each and every day of not having to bring a meal to work. Brown-bagging was just something I never got into the habit of doing.

The sergeant nodded his head, acknowledging I had purchased the toast. "I told him that each morning you buy breakfast and coffee, but he insisted it was state toast."

We both laughed at the foolishness of the conversation that just took place, and since he was just following orders, I didn't hold it against him. I did, however, hold it against the kiss-ass captain who visited the inmate area once in a blue moon to justify his job.

To illustrate his foolishness, I waited for the right time to play along with his childish games. It was many months later when my opportunity was presented to me like a gift. The Captain had been making his rounds and while discussing an issue, he began talking, in my presence, to the sergeant about an upcoming vacation for him and his wife. He took out his calendar book to verify he would be back from his vacation in time for the issue they were discussing. All officers carry a calendar book with them for a variety of reasons. We use the calendar books to track our time, and to know where we will be working and where we have worked. It's a record of events in case we are ever sued or called in for an investigation. We can then prove or disprove if we were even in the area of the incident in question.

Anyway, the Captain got called away on his radio and forgot his calendar book at my work station. When I knew he was out of the immediate area, I quickly looked at the two weeks of his vacation he had just spoken about. I was able to see not only when he was going, but where he was going, where he was staying, his flight plans and everything else about his trip, including confirmation numbers.

By the way, this was the same idiot who wanted to let all the reception inmates out to watch the Super Bowl many years before. And years ago, he had suspended a good friend of mine (George) and had terminated many officers for the silliest of matters, proving his loyalty to the suits on his way up the ladder to the rank of captain. Now it was be his turn to experience silliness from my handiwork.

A few of us got together and looked up as much information about him as we could find. This was the very early 1990s and long before technology blitz that gave us caller ID, cell phones and the internet, but we were able to come up with a few personal nuggets. Most of the secretaries couldn't stand him either, so they provided the personal information we needed.

We bought a calling card and went to work from a payphone at a local diner. We called the hotel and canceled his reservation and then called the airline and canceled his return flight. This way, he would arrive no problem, but then it would be quite the hassle to get a hotel once he landed, and he would have to find a new flight back. The airline asked for the reason and we said he had decided to rent a car and drive back. Who knows, maybe that's what he would have to do.

Knowing we made his vacation a bit of a bother, we planned a special treat for him on his return. With all the personal information we had gathered from the secretaries, we were able to contact the cable company, the phone company and the electric company. They were all notified that Captain Idiot was moving and we arranged to have all service terminated for the Friday he was supposed to return. His return trip would be completed by him entering a dark house with no phone to call anyone. Even if he went to a neighbor for the phone, there was no way he could get anything turned back on until at least Monday.

When he did return to work, as far as I know, he never mentioned any of it to anyone. He did, however, get the hint and never bothered any of us again. He retired a year later.

C.O., You Electrocuted Me!

I was a "rounds man" one day, meaning I was the one who brought the inmates from a reception part of the facility to a non-reception area where the rules are little more relaxed. The rules are the same rules, but not enforced the same way as in reception.

On this particular day, I escorted a couple of inmates from one area of the prison to another area, and while I was in that "more relaxed" part of the prison, I stopped by see a good friend of mine.

I was in the restricted "officer's only" area of the block when an inmate porter stepped over the yellow line, which was painted on the floor for a reason. I asked the inmate what he was doing and he gave me the line that all inmates give us. "It's okay C.O., the regular officer lets me do this."

My friend looked at the inmate and said, almost in an embarrassed fashion, "You know that you are not supposed to cross over that line."

Realizing that he just made the officer look bad, he quickly backed up and muttered, "My bad."

We all form relationships with certain inmates—inmates who are our block porters, inmates who work in our area on a daily basis, and inmates who we have known for years. For the most part, the inmates are just doing their time and don't cause any additional problems. But just like anywhere else, there is always that one percent that causes many of the problems we deal with on a regular basis.

This porter said he was sorry as a way to cover for my friend, and then he went on to state that his commissary date was not anytime soon and that his hot pot has stopped working. He explained that he was addicted and needed his coffee and that there happened to be an electrician on the unit fixing some overhead lights. He politely asked my friend if he could approach the electrician about fixing his hot pot. A hot pot is very important to the inmates because they use them to boil water, make coffee and tea, cook rice, etc.

We are not too thrilled with hot pots because the inmates heat up baby oil and other liquids they are allowed to have and then throw it on the officers. It's very similar to napalm in that it sticks to the skin as it burns and scars. The Department of Corrections will not outlaw hot pot use.

I intervened and told the inmate to make a "stinger" or "dropper," as it is sometimes called, like the ones the inmates made in Green Haven, many years ago when I was there. They would wind a piece of metal and connect it to a plug that they would then drop into a cup of water to make it boil. I asked him if he still had all the parts and he nodded that he did. We discussed it for a few more minutes and he said he would give a try that evening and that was that.

The next day I stopped by to see my buddy again and that porter walked up to me, smiling, and said, "Leo, you trying to electrocute me?"

I was at a lost at first, maybe because he was smiling and joking, but he followed me along the yellow line as I walked to the officers station so he could talk to both my friend and me. That's when he started telling us what happened evening before.

"I took the cord and stripped the wire down so that I could attach it to a piece of metal like *you* said," he emphasized, pointing to me. He went on to explain that he filled the now dismantled pot with water. He then put the plug into the outlet and dropped the piece of metal into the water.

"C.O., as soon as I dropped that into the water, I heard a big bang and all the lights on the tier went off and then the afternoon C.O. came walking down and started yelling at me. He said, 'What the hell are you doing in there. You just blew all the power on the tier.'"

"I told him that my hot pot had something wrong with it, and I think he believed me. He was pissed, but he opened the electrical cabinet and reset the circuit breakers for the tier. Then he stopped back by my cell and said if it happens again that the power would stay off."

Picturing this, we burst out laughing and continued to laugh because the porter re-told the story so well. "I didn't want to get in any trouble," he continued, "and I didn't want the other inmates to get pissed at me, so I thought about it for a while. I really needed my coffee, so I rewrapped the wire on the coil and hoped I wouldn't trip the circuit breakers again. This time, I dropped it in the water first and then plugged it in. I waited and nothing happened. The lights stayed on and I didn't hear any noise."

"So it worked?" I asked in between laughing.

"Well, Leo," he hesitated, "I wasn't sure. But you know how normally, if you want to see if water is getting warm, you stick your finger in the water to test it a little."

We nodded yes.

"Well, I stuck my finger in the water and my whole body started shaking and my teeth clenched." He started acting it out as he spoke, which only increased our desire to laugh. "I thought I was going to die," he said as he rattled and rolled, and stiffened and jerked, clenching his teeth. "I didn't know what to do."

My buddy and I were laughing so hard from watching him that our eyes were tearing. We all, at one time or another, have put our fingers in water to see if it is getting warmer, so now thinking that there were bare wires in that water and they were plugged in to an electrical outlet added to the near fatal comedy of the story.

The porter went on to explain that eventually he had to use his other hand to knock the hand in the water away from the pot, again acting out what he did as he told us. He was so sincere and good natured about it.

"There must have been something that I left out on how to make the dropper," I told him. "You know what? I will get you a new hot pot."

He was a really decent guy and I felt so badly that I went to the supply room in my area of the prison and rummaged through the "stash." The stash was a pile of miscellaneous items that had been left behind or had been taken from reception inmates for one reason or another. Normally, the stuff would have been thrown out, but some of it we saved for times just like this.

About ten minutes later, I returned with the hot pot and told him I was sorry for almost electrocuting him. Every time I would see him after that, we would laugh and he would thank me for the hot pot. That happened about fifteen years ago and to this day, I still laugh when I remember that inmate telling that story.

How Much Water Is in That Sink?

Some inmates are so violent at times that they are placed on a mechanical restraint order. This is fancy language that means the inmate must have handcuffs on whenever he is out of his cell. Normally, we would put him in handcuffs before he exits his cell by giving him the order to back up slowly to the door with his hands behind his back. Once he gets to the door, the inmate is ordered to squat down and stick his hands out the "wicket," which is a secured cut-out square in the solid steel door. Only when we see the wrists sticking out through the door will we place the cuffs on him. Then when we open the door and he is secured, we can check him for weapons without worry of being assaulted.

All inmates have bad days, as we all do. It's just that in prison the stakes are much higher. A bad day can mean anything from being in a bad mood to being in the kind of mood that starts a major disturbance. An inmate can be a model inmate for years, but we have to be on our guard for that one day when he can take us by surprise and revert to his violent ways.

This one inmate was not particularly known for trouble, but he had recently been placed on a "cuff order." We handcuffed him using the procedure I just described and escorted him to see the psychologist who had come to the unit to interview him. Because of privacy laws, we brought him to the interview room and left them alone. He spent about 45 minutes with the doctor, and when they were finished, the door opened and we were signaled to escort him back to his cell.

The steps for taking the handcuffs off the inmate run the exact opposite for putting them on. My partner and I opened the door and watched the inmate walk into his cell with no problem. We then secured the door and opened the wicket. This was his signal to back up to the door, squat down, and place his hands out the door so that we could remove the handcuffs.

The tricky part of this is that sometimes the inmates listen for the click of the first handcuff, and as soon as they feel it off their wrist, they quickly pull both their hands into their cell. The area we have to work in is so small and tight that we can't hold on without ripping the skin off the top of our hands, which I did a few times. This meant the inmate would then have one hand free, the cuffs and the handcuff key, which was still stuck in the first handcuff lock. He would simply use the key to open the second cuff. He then had something that is worth a lot of money in prison—the handcuff key.

Once the inmate is secured and that door is shut, we are not allowed to open the door without a supervisor's authorization. The inmates know this and have plenty of time to hide or pass off the handcuff key before we go through the bureaucracy of reopening his cell door to retrieve the key.

This inmate, for whatever reason, would not come towards the door and have his handcuffs removed. I ordered him over to the door and he just looked at us and shook his head indicating "No."

I told him if he didn't let us take off the cuffs, they would just stay on him, but there was no response. I finally said, "Keep them on…no sweat off our backs," and closed the wicket to signal to him that we were not going to wait all day for him to make up his mind. I'm not sure what was said in that psychologist interview, but it put him in some weird state of mind.

Then the most intriguing thing I ever saw in prison happened right in front my eyes. The inmate looked at us, smiled, and then stepped up onto his bed. With his hand still handcuffed behind him, standing on his bed, and he turned and started to stare down at the stainless steel sink unit about three feet away.

My partner and I looked at each other with widening eyes and thoughts of "Oh my god, he's going to jump." We banged on the door to get his attention and maybe snap him out of whatever was going on in his mind, and he did look over, but just stared at us.

We were both shaking our heads "no" and telling him to get down off his bed so that we could remove the handcuffs, when he slowly changed his stare from us to the sink again. And then he dove—head first—off the bed into the steel structured sink and toilet.

With no hands to break his fall, he landed on the concrete floor in no time. His forehead was split open and the blood was flowing at a pretty good pace on to the floor around him. We called to him, but he was knocked out, lying in a pool of his own blood.

We again looked at each other and I said, "Who is going to believe that a handcuffed inmate intentionally dove from his bed into his sink?"

Luckily for us, the nurse who had been on the next tier overheard us yelling at him to get down off his bed and walked over to see what was going on. She had been standing there most of the time and was a witness to the fact that we had nothing to do with a still cuffed, bleeding inmate sprawled on the floor.

Because of the medical emergency, we could now open the cell and let the nurse in. She tended to his injuries and had him brought to the hospital. We never did find out what in the world would be the catalyst to something like that. The inmate was transferred to an outside psychiatric hospital and I never got the opportunity to ask him, but I will always remember that something like this is possible.

Last Day at Elmira—Two Broken Arms

Four years of working in the Elmira Special Housing Unit was starting to wear on me, and I had filed my transfer papers a few weeks before. It was July 1992, and I had no idea this would be my last day there.

The daily routine began with no problems. I had my made my rounds and we had served the breakfast meal. Now it was shower time.

Since this was an SHU where the most dangerous and violent inmates were housed because they had committed some serious offense when they were out in general population, only one inmate at a time was allowed to be moved to any other place. Most of the inmates we were dealing with during the early 1990s were in the SHU for slicing other inmates with razor blades and many had the scars to prove it. This was the period of the gangs getting their foothold into New York prisons, and there was blood almost every day somewhere in the prison. It was called "razor tag."

We began moving toward the showers as we do every day. It's a highly synchronized process and involves four officers to complete safely. Two officers approach the door of the inmate who wants to take a shower and lower the observation window using a latch. As the steel plate swings down on its hinge, the inmate is easily visible. The officer then makes sure the inmate has no weapons in his hand before the door is opened.

In the Elmira SHU, we had too many incidents of inmates exiting their cells while hiding a cup of feces in their pants' pockets and then throwing it on the inmate we had already put in the shower. Since the inmates were never out together, this was their only opportunity to get at another inmate. As a result of this, we banned the wearing of pants to the shower. Each inmate would now exit his cell wearing boxer shorts and flip-flops, and carrying their soap and towel in their hands, which were firmly clasped behind their back.

If the officer on the door did not clearly see the inmate waiting by the observation window in boxer shorts and holding his towel, he would wait until this policy was complied with. I would wait at the shower area where three independent showers, each secured with a heavy gauge steel screen, awaited the inmates.

The officers on the door would let the inmate back out of his cell and then the escort officer would guide the inmate down the hallway to me. If the inmate removed his clasped from behind his back at any time and for any reason, the escort officer was to restrain him quickly and then we would converge from both sides to assist him. Otherwise, the inmate would walk into the shower stall and I would secure the door. Once the key was turned and the shower door was secured, I would signal that it was okay to send the next inmate.

During the time it would take for the inmate to walk down the hallway and into the shower stall, the door officers would go into the cell and do a quick search for weapons or contraband, as per Directive 4933. Since inmates in SHU were not out of their cells that often, we would use any opportunity that they were out to search it. They don't have much property in their cells, and that gave us the ability to move in and out in a speedy manner.

For whatever reason, things did not go according to protocol on that day. For starters, we had a new escort officer, who was walking the inmate in my direction when the inmate suddenly made a quick, dashing move back towards his cell. The escort officer did exactly as he was supposed to and attempted to stop the retreating inmate. I quickly ran down the corridor to help him and watched as the bolting inmate and escort officer began wrestling. Then I saw that the much larger inmate had the escort officer in a firm chokehold.

I was only a few seconds from helping the choking officer when I hastily thought about what I was going to do when I got there. Because of the way the inmate had the officer in the chokehold, I couldn't reach or grab his limbs to break the hold. The only target available to me was the inmate's face and head area. So as I raced towards the two, I decided that I would punch the inmate in the face as hard as I could, using all my forward momentum.

I clenched my right hand, making it into a fist, and committed to throw the punch toward the inmate's face. But just as my fist was about to make contact with the intended target, the officer being choked reached his one arm up in desperation. With a great effort to get the inmate's arm from around his neck, he moved the inmate just enough that I ended up punching the concrete wall behind them.

Their scuffle fell to the floor and I was now able to grab the right wrist of the inmate and place a pain compliance aikido hold on him. It created enough pain for him to release the other officer and make room for me to slide my grasp up the inmate's arm and now place him in a perfect arm bar. I continued to order the inmate to stop resisting and place his other arm behind his back.

The noise of the struggle got the attention of the other officer and the area sergeant, whom I could see running down the hallway to help with the struggle. Like I said, this whole incident lasted less than a minute.

The inmate didn't comply with my orders to stop resisting, so I slowly increased the pressure of the arm bar. Before I knew it I heard a loud "snap" and the next thing I knew, I was in possession of a limp arm. It took a second or so for it to sink in that the inmate's arm had twisted to the point that it broke.

At this point of my career, I had well over one hundred use of force incidents and had never broken anyone's bone before.

I immediately released my hold and watched as the inmate, now in shock, slumped to the floor and just laid there. Not being a security risk at this point, we quickly asked the officer who was being choked how he was. He said he was fine and my attention was now drawn to an aching pain in my right hand. In all the action, I had forgotten all about punching the wall, but when I looked down I immediately knew I had also broken my hand.

Ironically, both the inmate and I ended up at the emergency room of the Arnot-Ogden hospital with broken bones. We had the same orthopedic surgeon, and after he looked at both our x-rays, he said, "Who wants to go first?"

As the reality of having the entire summer of 1992 off on workmen's compensation, I quickly said, "Let him go first, I'm in no hurry."

While I was being examined, I was able to see the inmate's x-rays on that lighted white screen. I saw that I had twisted his left arm with so much pressure that it had snapped in two perfect cylindrical points. If you have ever placed a snapped dowel, with separate sharp points, back together to form a smooth round object again, then you have an idea of what his left humerus area looked like.

With a fresh white plaster cast on my right arm that also covered my wrist, I returned to the prison to file my reports. The mound of paperwork that I needed to prepare was typed by the superintendent's secretary, and I was unable to work for the next six to seven weeks.

The Boss Is Calling

One of the most amazing events in my career happened the next day when I was at home. The phone rang and when I answered it, the voice on the other end said, "Officer Leo? This is Superintendent Bartlett."

At this point, I had been a correction officer for eleven years and the only time I had heard of a superintendent even talking to a correction officer was to deliver bad news or to terminate the officer's employment.

"I heard one of the inmates down there in the SHU got a little out of hand yesterday and you broke your hand."

Again, being suspicious or thinking the call was being recorded, I replied, "Yes, sir."

"Well, I'm sorry you had to go through that and hope you get some enjoyment with your summer off."

Confused, I answered only, "Thank you, sir."

"We look forward to having you back in the SHU, so you get yourself better." And with that he hung up.

I was shocked, but it was something I always remembered. Now, as a union representative, I'm always amazed at the arrogance that came from many administrators I worked under and yet, this guy was the opposite. Most of the administrators forget where they came from or the mistakes they may have made along the way.

There was only one other person who stood out in this fashion and that was Deputy-Superintendent John Malloy. In my opinion, if the department could clone John Malloy and put him in every prison, there would be absolutely no administrative problems with the staff. Why? Because he listened. Regardless of your rank, he would ask for input as he made his rounds. Where the majority of administrators walk right by correction officers with their noses in the air, Deputy-Superintendent Malloy would gain insight from the men and women who actually worked among the inmates and performed the security functions.

There is a great lesson to be learned here for all of the administrators who are now reading this book, especially if you are constantly whining about the high workman's compensation levels experienced at your facilities. Start treating your front line officers as people and not numbers. When Superintendent Bartlett called me, asked me if I was alright, and then told me to enjoy my summer, I felt guilty for not being at work and I was the one who had a broken arm. Instead of being overly aggressive with the required paperwork from an injury, I did it without complaint. All an administrator needs to do is "act" like he cares, regardless of what they teach in their management school.

That was my last day working at Elmira prison, and I had the occasion to work with John Malloy at the Albany Training Academy many years later when I became a statewide union official. He had made the Academy a much more professional institution and had given it a better learning atmosphere. How did he do that? He listened and he cared.

John Malloy retired from the Department in the early 2000s, and unfortunately, to steal a line from Lloyd Bentsen, his successor is no John Malloy.

An Officer Assaulted Yesterday

For a couple of years, I had this one porter who was so well liked and trusted that even the "suits" who worked up front would use him to do different projects. He was an old white man and so well behaved, it forced me to ask him what he was in prison for. He said he was a thief and couldn't help it. He was honest and a great worker, but he told me if he were out on the street he would steal. He was so frail he could never hurt a fly, but would steal heavy machinery and anything else that wasn't tied down, as he put it.

Keep in mind that this was Reception and he should have been classified and moved out after 30 days or so, but he was one of those guys who everyone liked so much that his transfer was continually delayed so that he could stay at Downstate as long as possible.

During my regular two days off (RDO), various officers would be assigned to cover my work area. This particular area had the only porter job, and I handled all the inmate movement from that area.

When I returned from my two days off, I was standing in the roll call line up when the watch commander read a report on the previous days' events. This was done so we would all be familiar with the current atmosphere of the prison. We needed to know when and where problems had occurred so that we could be better prepared for the next day. For example, if we were notified of peculiar inmate groupings in the yard or gym areas, we would pay more attention to them and possibly stop something before it happened. Or at least, we'd know to call for help more quickly.

The Lieutenant continued, "There was an officer assaulted in complex 2 yesterday and the inmate is currently "keep-locked."

I remember thinking to myself, "That's my area. I wonder who it was and what happened?" In those days in reception, we didn't get that many officer assaults.

I made the long walk down the tunnel toward complex 2 with all my friends and co-workers. We then climbed the steep stairwell from the tunnel leading up to the complex and headed to our respective work assignments. My station was located right at the top of the stairs.

The first thing I did to begin my daily routine was get on the phone and start calling each unit for the names of the inmates who signed up for sick call. It always amazed me how many inmates would sign up for sick call simply to see what nurse was on duty. Then I looked on my desk and was surprised when I saw the large red keep-locked lettering over my porter's name.

I thought about the assault on an officer we had just been told about, and without even blinking an eye, I hung up my phone and walked through the gym and up the next flight of stairs that led to E-block, where holdover reception inmates were housed for various reasons.

I approached my porter's cell and saw him standing at the door. I looked at him and said, "James, just tell me what happened."

Inmate James appeared shaken when he looked at me. "Leo, I didn't do what she said I did."

I could see the misbehavior report, what we call a ticket, on his bed. "Let me see that misbehavior report she wrote."

He went to his bed grabbed the report and handed it to me. I looked immediately at the name and knew he didn't do it. I then read the report and knew something was strange. According to her report, she was walking up the stairs to the third level, and while this particular staircase is restricted to inmates, James had permission from the supervisor to be there to paint the walls. He was using a paint roller attached to a broomstick to reach the higher areas when, according to her report, she attempted to walk by. She said he "intentionally" used his elbow to strike her as she passed. She also stated that he used such force that paint from the roller sprayed all over her uniform sweater and she had to get a new one.

Something did not add up. I had known James for over a year now, and there was no way he would have done this. I had also known her for many years, and she, who was black, was not exactly pleasant to white people, let alone a white inmate. For years, she seemed to have a chip on her shoulders, and it was immediately clear that she had keep- locked this inmate for no reason other than that he was white.

I went to my area sergeant and told him that I didn't think James had assaulted her and he agreed with me. He said, "You know, she never even reported this to me yesterday. It was few hours later that I received a phone call from the watch commander, wanting to know why I didn't inform him that an officer had been assaulted in my area. I told him that no one told me about it."

Apparently, when the female officer went to get her lunch that day after the incident, she ran into the watch commander, who also happens to be black. Then she concocted her story about being assaulted.

Everyone was in shock, not so much because of the assault, but because of who the inmate was. The watch commander who was now on duty, who was white, looked over the report and also thought there was something suspicious in it.

Inmate James was immediately released from his keep-locked status, pending a full hearing, and I had James out of his cell and back to work within an hour.

During the next week, the sergeant, counselors and even the area lieutenant, helped inmate James prepare for his hearing. Inmate James was told what evidence to request and what questions to ask at his hearing. He was told to ask why she waited so long to report an assault, where were her medical reports showing any type of injury, and where was that sweater she claimed had paint all over it?

What we didn't know was that two counselors were coming down the stairs as she was going up the stairs, and because of the way the stairs are designed, the officer could not have known they were there. And since they didn't know she had submitted a report and locked the inmate up, they didn't even realize that they were key witnesses. Once they did, they immediately offered to help the inmate.

According to the counselor's statement, the officer had already gone by inmate James as he painted and had no problem with him. But when she got to the landing near the top, she yelled at him, "I'm sick and tired of all you honky mother fuckers." She then passed the counselors on her way to wherever she was going.

So there it was. No assault, no paint, no nothing. As a matter of fact, James told me that she had scared the hell out of him when she shouted at him.

A closed-door meeting took place at some point and all the charges were dismissed against inmate James and the Officer was reprimanded for filing a false report.

It was never discovered why she told the watch commander such a wild story other than the stress of walking around all day with that heavy chip she carries around on her shoulders. Most likely, she realized the counselors overheard her make her racist remarks to the inmate and now had to cover it up. But justice prevailed and James remained my porter for quite some time after that.

What the public would be most surprised to learn is that officers and inmates do develop relationships. We are together for many hours a day and it's inevitable. I'm not saying this is true for all of the inmates, but just like anywhere else, you find commonalities among large groups of people. Most inmates realize they made a mistake and they are doing their time. They don't cause any problems and don't want to encounter any problems either.

The one good thing that did occur during my career was the building of the SHU two hundreds. These are one hundred double-celled buildings where the inmates are secured in their cells for 24 hours per day. The worst of the worst of New York inmates are housed in these units, and it keeps the major troublemakers out of general population. These units have allowed the other inmates to do their time and go home.

Sick Call

Most inmates in prison sign up and go to sick call for one of three reasons. Don't get me wrong, there are some legitimate sick call cases, but many sign up out of boredom. They want to stare at the female nurses or slowly build a collection of medicines or both. The collecting of ointments is the usual item of choice, especially among the black inmates. They will claim that their skin is becoming dry and ashy. According to their claim, they will request and receive different creams and ointments. The most requested is the anti-biotic cream

Bacitracin. So while they are checking out the nurses and receiving their skin lotions, they are also compiling lubricants. That lubrication is later applied to wrists and arms and makes it very difficult to grab and restrain an inmate who is prepared for a violent outburst or to apply handcuffs.

Many times, when the inmate is aware some act of violence is going to take place in the yard, mess hall, or chapel, they will grease up in advance. They will also tape books and magazines to their bodies to negate inmates trying to assault them with razor blades or shanks. Did you ever hear the term "greased pig?" Imagine trying to restrain an oiled-up inmate who is fighting back or resisting your attempts to control him.

We had this very odd Jamaican inmate one time that had done just this. One day while making rounds, I noticed he had an unusual collection of chicken bones carefully arranged and stacked in the corner of his cell. He was standing in the middle of his cell with no clothes on and his skin was glistening from the overabundance of lotion and cream he had smeared all over his body. Having worked with this inmate for many years, I asked him if everything was okay. He gave me an evil smile, accompanied by a sinister laugh.

"You're all going to die, Leo," he said while he smiled.

"Yeah, yeah, yeah," I said.

"I mean today, Leo. You're all going to die today."

"What's up with the chicken bones?" I asked.

He charged towards the door. "Now away with you and leave me alone."

I called over the radio for my area supervisor and when he arrived on site, I explained what the inmate had said and how he was acting. The sergeant and I returned to the Jamaican's cell within a few minutes, and the sergeant immediately recommended to the inmate that he exit his cell and go speak to a psychiatrist over in the mental health unit.

With that Jamaican accent, he told the sergeant, "I told you, blood clot, you are all going to die. Now leave me be mun."

After several direct orders to exit his cell were refused, we assembled a team to extract him. I was the lead, and when the sergeant opened the cell door, we charged in.

What we had not seen was that the inmate had carefully attached saran wrap plastic across the door frame from end to end. He had pulled it so tightly across the frame that it was crystal clear, like when it's pulled across the lip of a bowl of fruit.

He had also smeared lotion of some kind on the saran wrap, which was later found to be Bacitracin ointment. He had vigilantly applied the lotion on the side that was facing us as we ran into his cell, so when the cell door is opened, we were startled as this sticky plastic adhered to our arms and faces. Sometime the inmates grease up the floor or string a wire so that you trip and fall as you run in, but this was a first.

The saran wrap didn't hinder us, but it did distract us because we didn't have time to figure out what it was until later. Nonetheless, we still tackled and wrestled the greasy inmate all as a part of the job.

I will never forget that evil smile. Nor the many thousands of society's most dangerous and evil faces of that I dealt with over the years.

Two Superintendents

I believe I am the only correction officer in the entire state of New York to have ever witnessed not one, but two superintendents (wardens) having feces thrown on them by inmates. The bout with first superintendent was well-deserved and necessary, which I will explain. The second one was just an incident where some dumb-kid inmate was trying to make a name for himself and the superintendent was in the wrong place at the wrong time.

The first superintendent was, in my opinion, one of the worst superintendents I ever worked under. Superintendent Bert Ross tried too hard to pamper and impress the inmates. I don't know, maybe he had some kind of guilt thing going. Anyway, whenever any higher-ups make rounds, they have to pass through different security stations on the way to their final destination. The first station puts out the call that the "brass is moving" or some other code so that everyone can be at attention and have things in order before they get to your area.

When the brass is coming, the coffee is put down and you make a quick round before he gets there. I had been working the "box," which is what they call the Special Housing Unit (SHU), for only a few months in 1989 when we got the call that Ross was "walking" our way. The Superintendent is required to visit the box every so often and we were used to it.

Each of us quickly walked one of the three galleries and made sure that each cell was in compliance with Directive 4933, the directive that regulates how the SHU is operated. We told each of the inmates to hide items that they were not supposed to have in their SHU cells, even the ones that the SHU sergeant allowed them to have. I remember each time laughing to myself that if the Sergeant we had at that time would just enforce directive 4933 on a daily basis, we would not have to go through this phony ritual.

Because of this lack of daily supervision, many of the inmates didn't want to leave the SHU when had finished their punishment. This particular supervisor would allow the inmates so much latitude that we looked foolish by going to each inmate and saying, "The Superintendent is on his way. You know what that means. I want all bed sheets back on the bed and not hanging on the bars for privacy. I need all the 'drag lines' pulled in and out of sight." Drag lines are the bed sheet ends that have been torn and tied to make a rope that the inmates use to drag or exchange items from cells to cell. These lines can be quite extensive and intricate so that an inmate in cell 1 could conceivably transfer a magazine or photo all the way to cell 54. "And put back anything else that is out of place," I said.

On this particular day when I approached cell number seven, this one inmate, whose nickname was "KK," was laying on his bed. He called out to me, "Yo, Leo, fuck that superintendent, I'm cold from the drafty air and I'm leaving my sheets up."

Sometimes this was said jokingly, sometimes the inmates are forced into it by other inmates, and sometimes they meant it. I heard the other inmates begin to shout out things like, "Yo, KK, you just a punk" and "KK woke up on the wrong side of bed today, Leo."

I slowed down my rounds and stood so that I was in front of number seven cell, but also so that the surrounding cells could hear me.

"KK, you know that before the Superintendent gets here, you will take the sheet down, so just take it down now so we can avoid any problems."

He stood up and said in a crazy whisper, "Yo, Leo, you see this?" Then he pointed to a Styrofoam bowl sitting on top of a Styrofoam cup. "I'm gonna shit down the Superintendent when he gets here."

Now, that had never, and I mean never, been done before. To even think of throwing something on a Superintendent was unheard of, so I responded with a, "Yeah, right, whatever. Just take the sheet down and pull in your drag line."

He said, "No, really. I'm gonna shit him down because he's an asshole." He moved towards the Styrofoam bowl and cup and showed me that he had caught a mouse and killed it. He had placed the dead mouse in the bowl and cut it open so that its guts could ooze out and into the cup below through puncture holes in the bowl's bottom. He was actually straining the blood and remnants of the dead mouse into the cup of urine and feces below to add a "kick" as he so eloquently put it.

I walked away saying, "KK, we all know you're not going to throw 'that' on the Superintendent. You don't have the guts to do something like that, so stop acting like you do."

By the time I was at the end of the tier, I had the thought—he's really going to do it. There was something in his eyes that day that was not normally there. Usually he was an alright guy.

Keep in mind, too, that many inmates had been throwing feces and urine on a lot of officers and Superintendent Ross had done nothing about it, the Department of Corrections had done nothing about it, and the Legislature had not yet made it against the law, which they did in 1994, some five years later. So at this point our attitude was, if we officers get feces thrown on us, so should the administrators. Only then will they understand.

I finished my rounds and found my two partners. I told them, "I think KK is really going to throw feces on the Superintendent." They looked at me like I was crazy. The thought of this happening was not comprehensible.

"Really," I repeated, "he really sounds like he's going to do it."

We all agreed to keep our mouths sealed, and if it did indeed happen, well, maybe then we would get some backing from our administration when cups of feces are thrown on us. New York State DOCS is a reactionary department and the administrators need to know what it feels like for themselves before the rules get changed. If they were proactive, this story would have never taken place.

The bell rang at the entrance of the Elmira special housing unit (SHU) and we instinctively looked up at the monitor. Through the wavy lines of the black and white monitor, we could see Superintendent Ross waiting to hear the buzzer on the solid steel door that would unlock it and allow him to proceed. Only after the officer in the secured control booth confirms the identity of the person trying to gain access to the box will he open the door. Once through the first door, a second steel gate is the next obstacle. It was here that we noticed he had someone else in a suit from Albany headquarters accompanying him.

As they went through the second gate, the two of them passed us by without ever even saying hello. Out of respect for the title of superintendent, we stood as mandated when they walked by. I was struck by the arrogance they both possessed and secretly hoped KK carried out his mission on both of them and not just the superintendent.

Anyone who enters the SHU must sign the logbook at the entrance door, so they went directly into the supervisor's office to speak with the sergeant. Then they began their rounds by walking up and down the tiers of the SHU. Never once did I think about warning these two suits of the impending danger they were about to encounter.

They started on the one through 18 tier, which meant they would be at seven cell very quickly. If there was going to be any excitement it would happen soon.

The three of us were now very curious as to whether KK would go through with his threat, and while we wanted to watch, we had to make sure we couldn't be seen. Otherwise, we would have been asked if we knew anything about it in advance and our presence might have tipped them off. So as we slowly approached the corner that looked down that tier, we situated ourselves like a totem-pole at different heights and peered down the tier. We listened to the inmates' voice their same old complaints about food and that's boring in the box, and so on. And as the brass approached ten cell I heard KK say, "Yo, Superintendent, I need to talk to you."

"That's why I'm here today. What's on your mind?" Ross replied.

"I don't want everyone else to hear my problem," KK said. "Can you come closer?"

The Superintendent made the rookie mistake of placing his face up the bars just as we all heard KK say, "This is what's on my mind mother-fucker!"

We then heard KK's evil laugh just as we saw Ross back up on his toes in a desperate attempt to avoid getting hit with that concoction of stench and disease.

But it was too late. KK had actually done it.

Superintendent Ross immediately threw off his jacket and ran down the tier towards 18 cell. That was lucky for us, because if he had run the other direction, he would knocked the three of over as he rounded the corner and he would have known that we knew.

We looked at each other and burst out laughing. When an inmate would throw feces or urine on one of us, we would always have to request permission from the sergeant to open the cell door and "talk" to the inmate about his misbehavior or "attitude adjustment.". And our request would always be denied.

I walked down to seven cell and KK was beaming with a great big smile, which quickly diminished. "They are going come in here and fuck me up, huh, Leo?"

"Not if you throw the cup out here on the floor. If you no longer have the cup, they won't have a reason to enter your cell," I said. "That's what they always tell us."

He dropped the cup out through his bars and I picked it up from the bottom with a paper towel and walked it over to the supervisor's office.

The Superintendent was standing at the door holding his suit jacket away from him with a look of pure disgust. He looked more upset that his jacket had been ruined than anything else. Then he and the guy from Albany went inside and the Sergeant closed the door. We just stood there staring at each other, hoping we didn't burst into laughter when they came back out.

Then the door opened and the Sergeant called us in as the two suits stood there silently, as the Superintendent continued to clean himself, using water and soap from the sink. "You have five minutes to enter that cell and secure that inmate," the Sergeant said.

Using the same line on them that we had heard numerous times I replied, "The inmate is secured sir. Why would we go in to his cell?"

The Superintendent looked at me and said, "To get that god-damned cup that he used to throw his shit on me, officer, that's why." We knew the Sergeant was under a lot of pressure to do something because the suits would somehow blame him.

"I have the cup right here, Sarge,I found it outside the cells on the 7-12 part of the tier. I added, I'm sure the Superintendent will be submitting a report since there were no other witnesses." I placed the feces cup in the wastepaper basket so they could see it and so I didn't have to keep holding it.

He looked at me like he wanted to rip my head off, but he knew I was right. I don't mean right in the sense of right or wrong. I mean right in the administration's convoluted sense of right and wrong.

The Second Superintendent

George Bartlett was the new Superintendent at Elmira by this time. He was a decent guy who would at least say hello to you when he entered your work area. I had worked at other prisons where the administrators would walk right by you as if you were an inmate. Actually, I take that back, they would acknowledge the inmates more.

On this day, I was making rounds on the front side of the tier three where cells 37 to 54 were located. We had placed all the feces and urine "throwers" in those cells because they had been specially fitted with steel-framed Lexan shields that were tight to the bars so that nothing could be thrown from the cell out onto the tier. We even had a specially designed cart made just to feed the inmates in these special cells so when we gave them their meals, they couldn't throw anything on us. Or so we thought.

If anyone is making rounds, we normally observe and listen to see what they are telling the inmates and what the inmates are telling them. And I would usually stand in a spot where they couldn't see me and wouldn't know that I was listening. And when the Superintendent got to cell 41, I heard him say hello to the inmate and then saw him back up in slow motion. He looked light a deer in the headlights as the shit hit, but then again there is no natural response to having feces thrown on you. You don't want to run down the tier away from the inmate. That just brings attention to what just happened and makes the inmates laugh. Having the inmates laugh at you every time you make rounds is the last thing you want.

Bartlett quickly got off that tier, but to his credit, he went the long way and did not come back my way, which would have gotten him out of there a lot quicker. In the animal world we gain respect in very primitive ways.

His first words were, "How the hell did it happen?" The inmate who the Superintendent pointed out as the one who did it was behind a shield welded to his bars. "He shot it out of his cell somehow," he shouted as he washed his face in the sink.

We looked at each other and I quickly went to the front side of the cell to figure out how he did it. The cell belonged to a dopey, harmless white kid named Joey, and as I lowered the observation window hatch, he was standing there with his face pressed up against it in an attempt to startle me. His nose was flattened against the small window and his breath fogged the glass. Then he smiled and backed away.

We know most of these guys on first name basis from spending hours, days and years with them. "Joey, what did you do?" I said, as I quickly scanned his cell to see how he propelled his feces onto the Superintendent.

To my surprise, Joey slowly removed his hand from behind his back, which was hiding a toothpaste tube. The look of confusion on my face prompted him to walk over to his stainless steel toilet, remove the cap and take aim at the water in his toilet bowl. When he squeezed the tube, a watery stream shot out.

He looked over his shoulder and smiled. He was quite proud of his invention. I must say I was impressed as well. The inmates' mind never ceased to amaze me. They had nothing but time to think about and invent just about anything.

I played dumb and acted like I didn't get it. His pride got the better of him and he carefully explained the whole process. The public might think the officers are cold and not caring, but we do form unique relationships of trust with many of the inmates. For the most part, they are doing their time and we are doing ours.

He showed me how he had wiggled the end of his empty toothpaste tube back and forth until it cleanly snapped off, like a beer tab. He then cleaned out any remnants of toothpaste from the empty tube with hot water from his sink. Then he screwed the cap back on and, having used an old Styrofoam cup to mix water and his feces, he poured the watery fecal liquid into the empty tube, filling it about three-quarters full. Then he slowly closed the opened end by bending the aluminum over two or three times, creating a tight seal. The tube, when uncapped, became a feces water pistol that was actually pretty accurate. The inmates' slang term for this weapon was "Uzi." When you heard an inmate utter, "Get the Uzi," watch out!

Joey, with his Uzi, was able to place the toothpaste dispenser end up to one of the holes in the plexiglass and squeeze the tube to propel the fecal water through the hole and onto the Superintendent at a distance of about ten feet.

I know the next question is, why there are holes in the plexiglass? By law there had to be holes for ventilation. Joey later told me that he never thought the

Superintendent would know where it came from and he was just having fun. This incident actually brought the seriousness and frequency of this disgusting act to the attention of Albany and it was eventually made a felony of aggravated assault.

It also led to using the "loaf" as a last resort punishment to curb the throwing of bodily fluids. The loaf is solid piece of bread with the daily supply of vitamins baked into it. It is then served in place of a meal. When it was introduced, the inmates hated it, and they complained that it was cruel and unusual punishment. The loaf was quite effective, but most administrators shied away from imposing this as a penalty because of outside pressure from some liberal groups. These are usually groups that have never worked in the prisons or experienced an inmate assault like having feces thrown on them. But if you ask them, they will tell you that they know better than those who actually work in the prison. Inmates manipulate these groups, take advantage of their liberal ideas, and intimidate the Department of Corrections through lawsuits. Unfortunately, those front-line correction officers have to deal with the liberal social experiments. Once one inmate figures out where he can manipulate the system, he informs the other inmates. Next thing you know no more loaf.

"Officer, There's an Apple in My Lunch"

While working in the box, one of my duties was to push the food cart down the corridor to the main kitchen and pick up the meals. Since this was the SHU, no inmate porters were authorized to leave the unit to do this. The directive mandated that the officer from the SHU personally observe the meals being prepared and loaded onto the cart. This was done so that the inmates in general population, who work in the kitchen, could not transfer contraband or hide weapons in a particular inmate's food and smuggle it into the SHU.

Some inmates have mandated diets prescribed to them by dieticians, doctors or for religious purposes. I had to make sure that those meals were included on the cart as well. Inmate Smith was one of these inmates who not only took advantage of the system, but would actually win each of his lawsuits. Smith was an older black guy who was physically harmless, but just a pain in the ass. He had a court order that we could not place handcuffs on him, a court order for his meals, and he even had a court order for the type of laundry detergent that had to be used when they washed his clothes at the laundry room.

One day, the inmate cook said, "C.O., I forgot an apple for inmate Smith's diet." He held one up.

I looked at the apple and made sure the skin had no punctures in it and let him place it in Smith's lunch container. Then I pushed the loaded cart back to the SHU and we began moving from cell to cell, delivering the meals the same way we do three times a day.

After sliding the container through the "feed-up" hatch, we would close the hatch and open the next one until all 54 inmates had been fed. We were about three cells past Smith's cell when he began yelling from his cell that there was something wrong with his meal.

I opened the observation window and saw Smith's scowling face holding the apple. "What the fuck is an apple doing in my meal?"

"Smith, that's what you're upset about?" I asked. "Throw the apple away if you don't want it. What do you want me to tell you?"

"Tell me why the fuck there is fruit in my meal?"

"Is that it? Anything else?" I said, not paying him much mind.

He smashed he apple against the window and with that, I closed the observation window and continued feeding the other inmates.

I had totally forgotten about the apple incident when, a week later, the Sergeant called me into his office and asked me if inmate Smith was given an apple. Apparently, inmate Smith had written the Superintendent about the apple being in his lunch and an investigation had been ordered and now need to be completed.

"You are kidding, right" was my first response.

"No, they want me to find out why he received an apple in his meal." The administration was in fear of another lawsuit from inmate Smith so they were jumping over each other to find out about the apple. I laughed as I thought about the time, money and resources they were expending to find out about that apple.

I explained that I had picked up the meals as I always did and I that I did not prepare the meals. The Sergeant then instructed me to write an official memo stating my involvement with the apple. The Department of Corrections loves those memos. So I followed the order and spent about an hour writing that memo and enjoyed my coffee.

On my next trip to the main kitchen, I asked the inmate cook if Smith was supposed to get that apple. He told me that he had already been questioned about the apple from the kitchen sergeant. He told the sergeant that he didn't know anything about an apple.

"I felt sorry for Smith," he whispered to me, "because his diet contained so little food, so I thought I would give the guy an apple." He laughed and said, "I will never do that again. That Smith is an asshole."

I smiled and nodded in agreement and pushed the loaded cart back to the SHU minus any apples.

Have You Seen My Keys?

The two most important things for correction officers are care, custody and control of the inmates and maintaining our keys. Nothing too difficult there, right? Our job is to count the inmates and make sure they don't escape. If they have the keys, they might get out.

Key control is taught over and over throughout our careers. So there is nothing scarier than that moment when you discover you may have misplaced your keys. It's like those two seconds when your toddler child is out of your sight and terrible images or thoughts race through your mind.

At the beginning of every shift, each officer receives a set of keys, either from the arsenal or the officer you are relieving. Regardless of whom you get the keys from, you sign for the keys and then the other officer has a receipt for those keys. Key control is corrections 101.

I was working at Downstate Correctional Facility in Dutchess County and one typical Saturday, I was making rounds around 7:30am. Normally, I worked only the east side of the complex's two main levels, but on weekends I was responsible to make rounds on the east side main level and the west side of the gym. The reason for this was that the west side officer was responsible for running the mess hall on the weekends. So while he was down at the mess hall, I would cover the security in his area.

Having done this for many years, I know what to look for, and I immediately noticed a large ring of keys still in a door lock down a hallway. This was an officer's only area on the west side of the gym. On the weekends, there was no one in this area except me and the west side officer because the gym was not in operation on Saturday or Sunday.

I approached the hanging keys, I immediately recognized them because both the east and west side officers have the same ring of keys. There are certain cuts to the keys which we become very familiar with after handling them for many years. So I pulled the keys from the locking cylinder and secured them on my key clip.

I looked in every room just to make sure that an inmate who wanted those keys had not heard me coming. I was concerned he might be hiding somewhere nearby, but once I was satisfied the area was secured, I continued my rounds.

I knew immediately who the west side officer was. We had worked together for many years and he was, in my opinion, emphatically the worst officer I had ever worked with. He was an older black man and was known to let black inmate workers and porters run his area for him. His leniency made all of our jobs much harder, because he would let the rules slide. Then we were the bad guys for enforcing the rules. Anyway, he was not very security conscience. And he had a black friend who was the watch commander, which the rank of lieutenant and this friend is looked out for him and saved his job many times.

I called the mess hall and asked a friend of mine if this officer was there. Even though he was worthless, he was still an officer and I needed to make sure he was okay. Once I verified that, I continued my rounds until the breakfast meal was completed.

Then I figured I would have some fun with him, and I placed the keys in a secured desk drawer. After the breakfast meal ends on weekends, we have about 15 minutes until all the inmates are let out to go to the yard. This key ring, which I also had, opened all the outside yard gates and gave perimeter access to whoever had those keys. I thought that in those 15 minutes he would realize he was missing the most important item that he was responsible for and make mention of it. I only let one good friend in on my secret, and we agreed to see how long it would take for this idiot to realize he is missing an entire key ring—a key ring that was quite large and heavy. Not something easily missed at all.

Complex two ran the yard from 9:00am until 11:30am on that day and still, there was no mention of the missing keys. This officer then ran the lunch mess hall, and still, nothing about those keys. Now it was time for the afternoon yard and around 2:15pm, he approached me and asked, "Leo, do you have my keys?"

His tone implied that I had done something wrong and yet he had lost his keys for the entire shift. Our shift was ending in 45 minutes and he was now accusing me instead of asking me. I should mention that if anything was going on in my area, everyone knew that I would know the who, what, where and why of what was taking place.

I was now agitated at his tone, his terrible security sense, and the fact that he could care less. "No, I don't have your keys, you have your keys."

"Seriously Leo, I need my keys." Here was this officer who was much older, had more time on the job, and who had come close to losing his job many times, telling me he needed his keys—which he lost and it only took him seven hours to realize were missing.

"I don't have them and I don't know what to tell you," I said. At that time the keys were in a drawer less than two feet from him, and while I was originally just going to teach him a lesson, I could see now that he could care less.

My buddy was nearby and looked at me and when the west side officer left the area, he said, "What are you going to do now?"

"Screw him," I said. "Let him deal with it." I then hid the keys in a supply room where I knew they would be secure and not fall into inmate's hands.

Not being able to find his keys forced this officer to make a call that no officer ever wants to make. He now had to inform the area supervisor that he lost the keys he had signed out and was responsible for since 7am that morning.

The area supervisor did not care for this officer either and simply asked him, "When did you last see them?"

He told him he couldn't recall and then the area sergeant notified the Watch Commander, yes his friend, that there were missing keys in complex two that had outside access.

By this time, it was about 2:30pm and the afternoon (3-11) shift was about to come on duty. The afternoon shift is typically smaller because there are fewer programs for the inmates to take part in after three o'clock. When the change of shift began around 2:45pm, the one officer, who knew about the keys, and I were walking down the tunnel towards the main building, which is where the time clock is located, and we could see many extra officers heading our way with metal detectors.

"What asshole lost the keys?" one officer jokingly asked.

Some of the day shift officers, who had volunteered for overtime, were smiling as they walked to the part of the prison we had just left. They were going to make some overtime money and could care less how long it took.

Once they passed us, I heard footsteps behind us and we turned to see who was there. It was him, the piece of shit officer who lost his keys, and he was also heading toward the time clock to go home, as if it was just another day.

I looked at him and said, "Don't you think you should help those officers who just passed us look for the keys that you lost? It might look good if you at least helped out."

Without a care in the world and with a shrug of his shoulders, he replied, "I ain't working no overtime. Let them look for the keys."

I shook my head in disbelief and went home.

The next day was Sunday, and when I entered the line up room, I saw him point at me and smile. I was more surprised to see that he was still employed, let alone pointing at me. He then pointed at his belt, which had one of those retractable key chains on it. He had gone out and bought the night before and was telling those around him that he was "Leo proofed."

"Do you have a problem?" I said as I walked up to him.

He just smiled, letting me know the alcohol rumors were true. So again, he pulled his chain and said, "I'm Leo proofed."

The unspoken rules in the Downstate officer's lineup room are similar to those in the inmate yard. The groups are broken up racially and everyone watches who talks to whom and listens to what is said. In front of the other black officers, he was making a statement. So I had to make mine.

I put my hand in his face and said loud enough for everyone to hear, "Let me get this straight, you are blaming me for you losing your keys?"

He just swayed and stared at me not saying a word.

"Go home, I can still smell that Johnny Walker is talking," I said as I walked away. I had to be careful not to cross the line where I could lose my job, but I also couldn't allow him to make it appear that I was somehow responsible for him losing his own keys. The good thing was that he had bought a key chain so that his keys would now be better secured to his belt. That was better for all of us and he had at least learned some lesson.

Later in the week, I placed the ring of keys in a place where they could easily be discovered by the sergeant, but not an inmate. We figured this would be the last straw for him, but according to our area supervisor, nothing happened. We were perplexed, but forgot about it.

It Happened Again

Exactly two weeks later on a Saturday, the exact same key ring was in the same exact door lock, just sitting there once again. The keys were there, exposed and unsecured.

I looked around and initially concluded that I was being set up. I looked in every nook and cranny because I was sure they had installed a camera in the area somewhere and that I was being watched. I just couldn't believe there was any way this idiot could do the exact same thing, especially after he proudly stated he was "Leo proofed."

I secured the keys and looked around. Then I looked again. I nervously searched for either a camera or some lieutenant hiding to see what I would do with the keys. Maybe he was angry that his watch commander friend got in trouble and he wanted to get even?

I tried to act naturally, in case I was being set up, and tried to think about it rationally as I broke it down in my head. I had been there all week. There were no construction teams in the area, and I would know if anything had been done differently or if anyone had hidden anything anywhere. I would have noticed if the sheetrock has been replaced. An inmate porter would have mentioned something at one point, since they can observe the area at night. I continued to mentally check my list. There was a different watch commander on duty so it wasn't his friend this time. Once I eliminated all possible scenarios, I came to only one conclusion: that dope had lost his keys again.

I secured the keys one more time and waited to see if he noticed this time. Same as last time, he didn't notice they were missing and he hadn't learned a single thing. Rumor had it that the first incident was never reported. This time, I told no one. I hid the keys in my jacket, punched out, and walked to my car.

On my way home every day, I cross the Newburgh-Beacon Bridge. It's a two-mile span across the Hudson River with a very small retaining wall. Needless to say, those keys were never found and they are very safe, deep below in the muck of that historic river.

Unfortunately, that officer was not disciplined either time for losing his keys because his friend allegedly intervened on both occasions. Anyone else would have been terminated or at least brought up on charges.

Take Your Clothes Off

"Make sure your block is secure and report to B-Block as soon as you can." That was the order I received from my area supervisor one evening when I was working the 3-11 shift. I was on the reception block so I double-checked all the doors of the cells. In the evening after dinner, the inmates do not come out of their cells for the first 30 days at Downstate. Once I was satisfied that everything was locked down I walked next door to B-Block.

When I entered the block, I noticed the lights in the dayroom were turned off and that there was one inmate standing there in the middle of a circle of officers. There was also one visible white-shirted sergeant. I had no idea what was going on, but quietly made the circle larger by one more body. I had never been asked to participate in something like this before, but I had heard stories. As a 22 year old, I was still at the age where I wanted to be part of the "group," but quite honestly, I didn't know what that entailed.

Apparently, there was this one particular inmate who liked to masturbate in front of the female officers on the day shift, and word was passed on to straighten him out. The Sergeant was an old timer and acted like he had done this many times as he spoke to the inmate while we surrounded him.

"So you like to play with yourself around the females?" he asked with his baton in hand.

The inmate was standing his ground, but concerned.

"Start getting undressed" he told the inmate.

The inmate started to respond but barely eked out a "but," when the Sergeant cut him off. "BUT NOTHING," the Sergeant shouted. "Either you get undressed or these officers will do it for you. You make the choice"

Many of us knew each other, but before this, we had not spoken about what had happened or what was going to happen. There was no pre-planning. We looked at each other for clues and basically had to be prepared to do whatever we were told to do.

The inmate slowly removed each article of clothing from his body as he nervously looked over his shoulder. Once he was fully naked, the sergeant took his baton, raised it, and asked the inmate what he thought it would feel like if he hit him as hard as he could in his "private area" with the baton?

"It would hurt. It would hurt a lot sir," he said.

"Don't call me sir! I work for a living," the Sergeant quickly snapped back.

The inmate nervously stated he would never bother another female staff member again and that he was sorry. Tears came down his face and he kept saying he was sorry. This went on for a minute or two.

Then the Sergeant barked another order. "Get your clothes on."

We stayed put and just watched and figured the mind game worked and it was over.

Then the Sergeant spoke again. "As you're getting dressed, I want you to look around at the officers here and decide which one you're going to fight. One-on-one and no one else will jump in. I want to make sure you get all your aggression out tonight."

We looked at each other and luckily the lights were off or the inmate would have seen how nervous we were. And I will never forget the expression of the officer next to me, thinking he may be picked.

"Please, Sarge, I don't want to fight no one. I don't want any trouble," the inmate said through his tears.

"Too late. You already found trouble."

The inmate was now fully dressed and kept his hands in his pockets to clearly indicate that he was in no way a physical threat. He was surrounded by six officers with their batons drawn and he didn't want to give any false indication of an aggressive action. He continued to apologize to the sergeant and promised he would never be any trouble again.

"So, if I let you go back to your cell, you are telling me and these six officers that you will never be a problem again?"

"Yes, Sarge, I promise."

"Go lock in, then," the Sergeant told him.

We watched as the inmate walked back to his cell with his head down and his hands in his pockets. The aggressive inmate had just been made submissive without any physical force. This was the first and only time I had ever seen or been involved with something like this, but it worked.

I Need Your Keys

I haven't named too many names in this book, so I will refer to this female correction officer as the Big Betty. We have many great female officers that come to work and do their job, but we also have a few that report to work and don't want to work. They will use their feminine abilities to weasel their way out being assigned to the more dangerous areas of the prison. How does this work? Simple, the supervisors assigning the jobs are men.

Over the years, the Big Betty reported to work and rarely was assigned to work "down back" where the inmates were. She was about six foot in height and had manly features, very much like a woman bodybuilder type. For some reason the Superintendent had taken a liking to her, and over the years she received special assignments, like giving new employees a tour of the facility. For those of us that worked down back and put our time in working in the dangerous areas, this was a slap in the face. How can you have someone give a tour in front of their peers who rarely works in those areas themselves?

One day the Big Betty entered my area from the tunnel control area. She walked up the stairs with an outside group of contractors. Many times, outside maintenance contractors are subcontracted to fix problems that cannot be repaired internally.

As she pointed where the outside contractors needed to go, she walked toward me and said, "Leo, I need you to open the women's bathroom for me."

"I don't have the keys for the bathroom," I replied.

"I know you have the keys, Leo. Just give them to me."

"If you worked down back more often," I retorted, "you would know that I do not have the keys you are looking for. But if you really need to use the restroom, there is a bathroom upstairs or there is another one right down stairs in the tunnel control area where you just came from."

"Come on Leo, just give me the keys."

I repeated that I didn't have them and she walked away. I figured that was the end of that. Boy was I wrong. What happened next illustrates how absurd the Department of Corrections has become when it comes to issues like this.

The following day, my union representative called me at my work location and told me that the Superintendent wanted to see me in his office immediately. Normally, we wouldn't see a Superintendent for months at a time and that was only if he got up enough energy to take his fat ass off his office chair to take a tour. The Superintendent has to walk around every once in a while to justify his position. So what they do is sign the logbooks around the facility and then return to the safety of their offices. This way when Albany suits take a tour, they will see that the facility superintendent has been making his rounds.

My relief appeared. "Leo, 'Fat-ass' wants to see you."

I made the long walk up to his office, trying to figure out what in the world he wanted to see me about, and when I open the door, I immediately saw Big Betty standing there with a large grin on her face.

Corrections is a para-military organization that follows a strict chain-of-command protocol. She had the luxury of going right to the top. Why?

The Superintendent remained seated and as I entered the room, I noticed the only other person there was the same union representative who had called me earlier.

"Officer Leo, is it true that you refused to give your keys to Officer "Betty" yesterday when she needed to use the restroom?"

I looked at him in a way that quickly signaled to him that I thought this was a joke. With a big smile and knowing I did nothing wrong I said, "No."

"Yes, he did Tom, I mean Superintendent," she said.

Like a man protecting his daughter, he waved his hand to calm her hysterics. "Officer Leo, did she ask you for your keys?"

"Yes," I nodded.

"And did you give them to her?"

"No"

"Okay, why not?"

I started with the facts. "Sir, she entered my area at 1:15pm. If you check the log book in the tunnel, it clearly states that she entered the tunnel area at that time and then into my area. According to my official job description, which I have been following for many years now, I turn my keys over to the 1-9pm officer at 1:00pm. This is required so that the 1-9pm officer can open the secured recreation area for the inmates on 'keep lock' status to get their one hour of mandated exercise. The 1-9pm officer maintains possession of my keys for one hour during this time. This officer entered my area at 1:15pm and requested the keys. I told her I did not have them, and I have just explained to you why I didn't. You can also check with the 1-9pm Officer, if you want."

My union representative smiled, but "Betty's" eyes were bulging open as if she wanted to scream.

The Superintendent looked down at the papers on his desk and made some notes and then said, "Okay, Officer Leo, that will be all. You are dismissed."

I exited his office, excited that I had logically explained the foolishness she had begun and the foolishness the superintendent's testosterone had fed into.

When I returned to my work location, I received a phone call from my union rep, telling me that while he was still in the office, Big Betty had pleaded with Fat-ass to do something. My rep said that he told her there was nothing to do if that was indeed what my job description stated and what I had done. He said he would review my job description and check the tunnel logbook, but if all holds true, the only other thing he could think of was for her to initiate a sexual harassment claim against me and my actions.

"What does that mean?" I asked my rep.

"That means you are in big trouble, Leo," he said. "They take that harassment stuff very seriously and she is a woman and they will probably take her side."

This didn't make sense to me at all. I was right and yet I'm still in trouble? "What should I do?"

"The Superintendent told her to go meet with the employee assistance program representative to file the claim. That means you have some time to figure something out, but in my experience whoever puts a claim in first wins their case."

I received a call from the training officer a little later. His office was right next to the EAP office and he quickly informed what was going on based on what he overheard. The most important thing he told me was that the EAP rep advised her to take her time in preparing her report of sexual harassment and to make sure it was something that would stick. This occurred on a Friday and I figured Betty would take the weekend to work on her claim, so I had to do something before then.

Remembering what he said about being the first to put in a claim, I went into action. One of the rulebooks we have to abide by is the employee's manual. It covers everything from what you do on your personal time all the way to how you use toilet paper. In the employee's manual there is a section about sexual harassment and the penalty is termination. With my job and pension on the line, I couldn't take the chance that some bureaucrat would listen to me if the Superintendent didn't.

I called three of my closest friends and asked them each to write a memo stating that they had observed or heard the Widow sexually harass me in the last few weeks. I also had to call the EAP rep and ask for a sexual harassment form. This was delicate because I didn't want to tip her off on what I was doing because she would tell Betty. I told her I was picking up the form for someone else and she quickly gave it to me.

Directly in front of my workstation was a group of civilian counselor offices. They couldn't stand Big Betty either, and after I informed them what she was attempting to do, they offered any help they could. One of them even offered to write a memo that she overheard the conversation about the keys. In the prison setting, a civilian's word has more power than an officer's, so I gladly accepted.

I filled out the official sexual harassment form and gathered all of my "witness" memos. I noticed a fax number on the form, and since I was in a hurry to get my complaint in first, I accepted the counselor's offer to use their fax machine. Just like that, my complaint was in before Big Betty's and it was now official. Anything she now submitted would simply appear to be a reactionary response to protect her from my charges.

A few weeks later, we had both received some letter informing us of the complaint and the date of the hearing. Word quickly circulated around the facility that I brought Betty up on sexual harassment charges. Officers that I rarely spoke to were giving me the thumbs up and wishing me luck. I was now safe from her and the Superintendent because anything done to me from this point forward would be retaliatory for my complaint and Fat-Ass knew he could get in some major trouble for that, regardless of his testosterone.

The hearing date was set and as we approached my Day of Judgment, she spoke to one of my supervisors and asked him to speak to me about withdrawing the charges because of the consequences, which was termination.

"Look Leo, you made your point and I think she has learned her lesson," he said. "Why don't you withdraw the charges of sexual harassment and let it go?"

I told him I would think about it and get back to him. I contemplated all the different outcomes and knowing her past, my major concern was that if I withdrew my charges, she would probably continue to pursue her complaint. I could not take that chance.

And then a stroke of genius hit me. I called the Supervisor and said that I would indeed drop the charges. This way he would go back and tell her that I withdrew the charges and she would be unprepared for the hearing.

The hearing went forward and the representative from Diversity Management arrived on the scheduled day and my area supervisor notified me that I was to report to the Superintendent's office. Fat-ass had kindly offered his office for the hearing. Wasn't that nice of him.

I entered the office and the first thing I observed was the woman from Diversity Management and Betty chatting and laughing. I thought to myself, I don't have a prayer. The Superintendent excused himself and he had the audacity to wish Big Betty "good luck" in front of me as he left.

The door shut behind him and the hearing officially began with an explanation of the guidelines of the hearing process. Then the Hearing Officer directed her first question to Betty.

"According to Officer Leo's statement and the statement of his witnesses, you have approached Mr. Leo on many occasions and asked him to meet you out for drinks. Mr. Leo has repeatedly turned you down, but you have become more insistent over time. How do you respond?"

Being a very tall and muscular woman, she stood in anger and began her answer with a statement instead of a simple yes or no. "First off, I would need a step-ladder to date Officer Leo. Do you see the size of him?"

I quickly interrupted and acted as if I was appalled at her making fun of me and the fact that she was much larger than me. I turned to the hearing officer and continued to illustrate the absurdity of this entire process with just a look on my face.

"This is exactly the type of harassment that I have been putting up with from her and I will tolerate it any longer," I said. I'm not sure if I was more stunned by the fact that Betty made such a stupid remark or the fact that the hearing officer actually believed me and agreed with me.

The hearing officer nodded her head as she turned to my "harasser" and told her, "I will not tolerate any remarks like that and you will refrain from those types of comments during this hearing. Do you understand me?"

While Betty shook her head in acknowledgement, the hearing officer looked down at her folder and made some notes. Big Betty and I looked at each other and I put a big grin on my face, quickly rubbed my two index fingers at her, and mouthed, "naughty, naughty." This infuriated her and she was off her game for the rest of the hearing.

I also introduced copies of my job description and the tunnel log book page from that day, proving that Betty was strictly retaliating for me rebuffing her advances. I also had it put in the notes that the Superintendent was "chummy" with Betty, and I was worried about the two of them cooking up another scheme to terminate me. I was reassured that my concerns would be recorded and that I had nothing to worry about should that occur.

When we finally stepped outside to await the hearing officer's decision, Big Betty looked down and saw my three witnesses in the hallway. It may have been from tension of the hearing and not having it go to well for her or the fact that my three witnesses were there if I needed them, but she became hysterical and screamed, "You said you were going to withdraw you charges."

I just ignored her and looked at my friends a few feet away. I made the circular motion with my right index finger near my temple indicating to my smiling witnesses that she was cuckoo. She huffed a bit and then the door opened.

"Will the two of you please come back in?"

We followed the hearing officer back to the table where she had just heard our testimony.

"Officer Leo, there are four sections of dispute here and I have found in your favor on three of them."

I had a look of bewilderment on my face as she continued. "The fourth section is about the keys. If any officer asks you to use the restroom, you are to give them the keys."

My job description, which she just read, clearly states that I didn't have the keys and I was amazed at how retarded this affirmative action representative was, but kept my mouth shut and signed the agreement.

I exited the office, gave the thumbs up to my friends, and proceeded directly to the copy machine. I made hundreds of copies of the agreement and handed them out at the time clock, telling everyone that they no longer need to walk on egg shells around Big Betty. I got more accolades for that victory than I ever received for taking a weapon away from an inmate or for responding to a red-dot situation. Times certainly have changed in prison.

Fact vs. Fiction

*New York State Correction Officers DO NOT carry guns. Let me repeat that. Correction Officers DO NOT carry guns. We watch sixty or more inmates by ourselves with nothing but a pair of pants, a shirt and sometimes a baton. As you can see, the baton is only for defensive reasons. If sixty inmates decide to take that baton away from you it's over!

*New York State Correction Officers DO NOT carry pepper spray or mace into the prison. In New York State we are trained in its use, but never ever use it. The officers in the towers do have it, but it's very rarely authorized to be used.

*New York State Correction Officers DO NOT wear helmets and vests. Our only source of protection is our mind and verbal skills just like anywhere else. It's kind of like going into a war and your company commander says, "Men, the

General has decided that we no longer need our rifles, so go get em, but be safe." The only difference is that we deal with one-hundred percent of convicted felons.

* You must be tough to be a Correction Officer. NO, we are outnumbered everyday so you must be smart to be a correction officer. We do however become tough minded through years and years of being challenged mentally by the inmates and the administration. We are challenged by the best of the best when it comes to mind games. Some survive and some don't. Those of us that do survive retire as soon as we can.

*We   DO NOT   beat inmates. I will readily admit that many, and I mean many, years ago if an inmate got out of hand or refused a direct order we used force to control the situation. Today, not only is using force very rare it is also not worth the time and effort unless your life is in danger or you are about to be attacked. When I began my career if an inmate refused to go into his cell it was simple, you put him in his cell. Over the last twenty years or so, Building two in Albany has slowly taken all administrative responsibility away from the individual facilities and most decisions are now made from their "command center" located in their massive operations center staffed with hundred's of highly paid employees. The micromanaging of the facilities by "building number two" has inadvertently proven the point that the seven to ten layers of administration at each of the sixty-nine prisons could easily be done away with or at least consolidated. Today, if an inmate refuses to go into his cell you have to contact your sergeant. The sergeant will alert the watch commander (Lieutenant). The watch commander will call the captain. The captain will contact the deputy-superintendent of security (DS) the DS will make a phone call to the colossal operations center in Albany. While some overpaid bureaucrat looks through the master records of the inmate who is refusing to enter his cell. The "Command center" in Albany will check the files and see if this inmate has any medical problems, any psychological problems and what his disciplinary record looks like. Meantime, at the facility level all efforts to avoid using force are in motion. The local facility administration will have a civilian counselor plead with the inmate to lock in. If that doesn't work they will have someone from the spiritual or religious sector speak with the inmate to see what is bothering him. There was even one time they allowed the inmate to call home and speak to his mother if he agreed to then lock in his cell peacefully. Once Albany makes their "command" decision they will reverse the chain of command. The DS will be made aware of how the inmate should be handled. He will let the captain know what Albany has decided who will then get on his phone inform the watch commander. This could take hours and you may have already gone home by the time the "decision' is made. The watch commander will radio the sergeant and everyone is waiting to see what the geniuses have decided. Many inmates will do this just see who can tie up the chain of command with this silliness. The correction officer knows the game and just goes about the rest of his or her duties ignoring the whole situation.

*Aren't the inmates locked in all the time? NO. Actually it's the exact opposite. New York prisons run exactly the opposite as what you see on television and the movies. In New York prisons you have to keep in mind that of the sixty thousand inmates, thirty thousand of them are medium security inmates. That means one-half of New York State prison inmates are never locked at all. They live and sleep in dormitories. There are no bars, no cells and no doors to secure. In many instances the department of corrections has built double-bunk beds for the inmates. This way there can be even more inmates cramped into the dorms and still with only one officer. In the maximum security prisons the inmates are usually locked in to be counted and to sleep. Inmates are out all day going to the gym, mess hall, library, watching television, barber shop, school, work, learning a trade, yard, going to the store etc… Of course this would not apply if an inmate is locked in for disciplinary reasons. In the medium facilities if an inmate is on a disciplinary it is called cube restriction. The officer has to say, "Don't leave your cube because you are restricted."

*Do the inmates eat bread and water? NO. The inmates are very well fed. There are dieticians that prepare the menus and all meals include juice, fruit and desert. Of course there are special meals prepared for those inmates on a diet for medical or religious reasons. Each inmate can also buy food at the commissary and receive packages from friends and family members. Many inmates never even go to the mess hall because they have so much food in their cells. Having eaten "state food" on many occasions of mandated overtime, I can say with extreme confidence that inmates are very well fed.

*Aren't the inmates cells searched every day? NO, as a matter of fact the inmate's cells are barely searched. Each block officer is given a random cell search form each morning for three (3) cells. The block officer nowadays has such limited time and staff to assist that very often the officer does not have the ability to do the cell search properly. The administration thrives on keeping and compiling data. The act of completing the form has become more important than the actual cell search itself. Many officers have to fill out the form as if the search had been completed as way of covering themselves. In the reported data it may appear that level of contraband is down, but it's just because we are not able to search the cells properly ,if at all. The forms will be turned in as if the search was done and it will read, " No Contraband Found " (NCF). And this way you don't get in trouble for not turning in the form. Everyone is happy including the inmates, just like the administration prefers it to be.

*I hear a lot about prison rape. How often does it happen? I have to admit that in my twenty-five year career I have never seen or heard of it happening. I have asked many co-workers over the years and have yet to find it occurring. That doesn't mean it doesn't, I have personally never seen or heard of it.

*Gangs in prison don't exist?   False.   The New York State Department of Corrections refused to admit that gangs exist in prison until only the last few years or so. They felt that if they ignored the problem it would go away. When it comes to dealing with gangs New York is way behind the eight ball in both their training and their ability to identify potential problems. Gangs do exist in New York prisons and they are just as dangerous and ruthless as you can imagine.

Twenty-five and out!

Correction Officer's Prayer

The Correction Officer stood and faced his God, Which must always come to pass;

He hoped his shoes were shining, just as brightly as his brass.

"Step forward now, officer, How shall I deal with you?

Have you always turned the other cheek?

To my church have you been true?"

The officer squared his shoulder and said, "No, Lord, I guess I aint, Because those of us who carry badges can't always be a saint.

I've had to work most Sundays, and at times my talk was rough, and sometimes I've been violent because the prisons are mighty tough.

But I never took a penny that wasn't mine to keep, though I worked a lot of overtime, when the bills got to steep.

And I never passed a cry for help though at times I shook with fear and sometimes, God forgive me, I wept an unmanly tear.

I know I don't deserve a place among the people here; they never wanted me around except to calm their fear.

If you've a place for me here, Lord, it needn't be so grand, I never expected or had too much, but if you don't...I'll understand.

There was silence all around the throne, where the saints often trod, as the officer waited quietly for the judgment of his God.

"Step forward now, officer, you've borne your burdens well, Come walk a beat on heaven's streets, you've done your time in hell".

Author Unknown

NEW YORK STATE DEPARTMENT OF CORRECTIONAL SERVICES FACILITIES

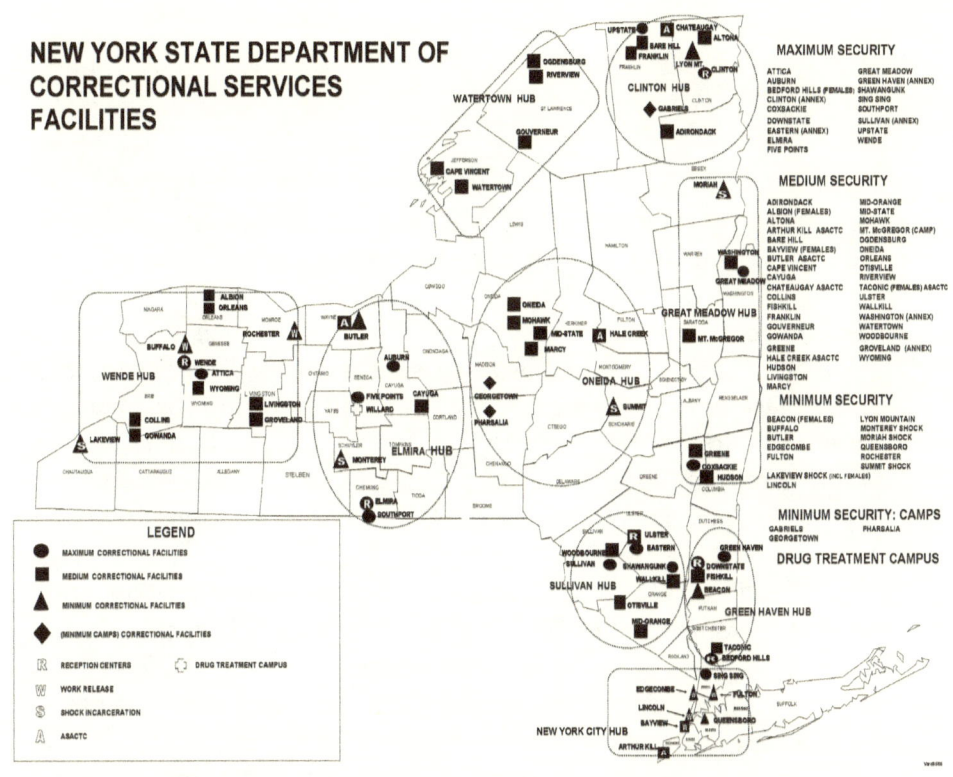

Map courtesy of NYSDOCS

For additional information concerning New York State Correction Officer's, please visit
www.NYSCOPBA.org   or   www.ChristopherLeo.com

About the Author

Chris Leo has a diverse twenty-five year background, vast experiences and expertise in the field of corrections and use-of-force. While working in three of New York's maximum-security prisons Mr. Leo became a Master Instructor and completed the following training courses: Train the Trainer Instructor Course , Unarmed Defensive Tactic Instructor, Advanced Defensive Tactics Instructor , Video Operator Certified, Syva EMIT-st Urinalysis Instructor, Advanced Special Housing Unit Instruction, Tunnels and Rooftops ,Video Operator recertification, Corrections Emergency Response Team (CERT) Certified, Advanced Corrections Emergency Response Team (CERT) Certified, Unarmed Defensive Tactic Instructor Recertification, General Topics Instructor Recertification, MPTC Instructor Evaluator Certification, Blood-borne/Airborne Instructor , Master Instructor – Narcotics Identification, Inappropriate Behavior Instructor, Aggravated Harassment Collection Instructor Course. Mr. Leo is also an expert witness in the 'use of force' in the State of New York. Mr. Leo is currently pursuing his Masters Degree in Political Science.

ChrisLeo.Leo@Gmail.com

ISBN 978-0-557-15507-1

www.ingramcontent.com/pod-product-compliance
Lightning Source LLC
Chambersburg PA
CBHW031321290526
45784CB00014B/558